COMMUNITY CARE ASSESSMENTS:

A PRACTICAL LEGAL FRAMEWORK

COMMUNITY CARE ASSESSMENTS:
A PRACTICAL LEGAL FRAMEWORK

RICHARD GORDON

Barrister, MA, LLM
Helena Normanton Prizewinner
in Administrative Law

Foreword by

The Honourable Mr Justice Sedley

Dedication

For Bunny

© Richard Gordon 1993

ISBN 0 75200 0268

Published by
Longman Law, Tax and Finance
Longman Group UK Ltd
21–27 Lamb's Conduit Street London WC1N 3NJ

Associated offices
Australia, Hong Kong, Malaysia, Singapore, USA

A CIP catalogue record for this book is available from
the British Library.

Printed in Great Britain by
Hobbs the Printers Ltd, Southampton

CONTENTS

PART 3   LEGAL REMEDIES

PART 4   FINANCIAL ASPECTS OF ASSESSMENT

FOREWORD

The new regime for community care offers a range of opportunities and a range of pitfalls. Its fundamental characteristic is that it is a legal regime, containing within it a series of duties, discretions and judgment calls, but bounded and shaped by law. The growth and sophistication of modern public law, through the processes of judicial review, now mean that a statutory regime cannot be understood simply by reading the statute: the common law made by the judges can be called in to investigate the fairness and legal propriety of what local and central government do as they seek to implement legislation.

It would be a great pity if the presence of legal controls were to lead to defensive and opaque decision-making, and there is no reason why it should. Reasoned decisions conscientiously taken in conformity with the law will not only avoid the time- and resource-consuming ordeal of judicial review; they will be better and fairer decisions.

Richard Gordon's book is thus not primarily a battle plan for lawyers, though it will certainly enable lawyers to get a sound grasp of the legislation and to advise clients about their entitlements. It is a guide to sound decision-making. The principles of fairness and legality which the law attaches to decision-making powers, especially those which touch people's most basic needs, are not an obstacle course designed to trip the unwary. But they do require knowledge, information, advice and forethought, and none of these comes easily in relation to a scheme as innovative and as complex as that which came into force on 1 April 1993.

By enabling administrators and decision-makers to do their sensitive jobs within the law, then, this book will primarily contribute to sound public administration and through it to responsive community care for some of the neediest people. But secondly, by furnishing lawyers with the information they need to assure respect for people's entitlement to fair and lawful decision-making, it will provide the back-up without which rights are fruitless and obligations hollow. Properly understood, the two functions are complementary, not antagonistic, and it is the strength of Richard Gordon's work on the legislation that it serves both functions equally. His own high standing as a specialist writer, adviser and advocate in the field of public law, and especially in the area of social services, makes this an authoritative and dependable book, an aid for the needy and a significant contribution to government within the law.

Stephen Sedley

PREFACE

This short work is intended as a practical legal anatomy of the new assessment regime introduced by s 47 of the National Health Service and Community Care Act 1990.

Although community care assessments do not alter the substantive law, it is clear that transfer of responsibility to social services departments for the assessment of need and the provision of community care services will give rise to many legal problems. These include, most importantly, the practical issues as to how a local authority's assessment, service provision and complaints procedures are to be regulated and conducted fairly and lawfully, and how financial assessments are to be carried out. The large attendances at conferences on community care clearly demonstrate the need for assistance with these problems.

Guidance, circulars and directions emanate almost daily from the Department of Health and other government bodies. In the face of this almost overwhelming material the practitioner can feel confused; even helpless.

This book summarises as simply as possible most of the important material and provides practical help in the form of precedents and extracts from the relevant statutes and guidance. It progresses logically by dealing first with the criteria for assessment and service provision, then the requirements that the law imposes as to fairness. Finally there is a section on legal remedies and the financial implications of assessment.

It is hoped that the approach adopted will prove helpful to those lawyers working in local authorities and in private practice. In preparing the text, at some speed, I have had help and support from members of my chambers and from Paul Ridout at Nabarro Nathanson and Janette Bird at Birmingham City Council. My wife, as always, has been an unfailing source of support. Craig Barlow, my former pupil, wrote the chapter on financial assessment (Chapter

11) with his customary speed and legal excellence. The law is stated as at 1 April 1993. Any errors are entirely my fault.

Richard Gordon

39 Essex Street, London WC2R 3AT
1 April 1993

TABLE OF CASES

Table of Statutes

Table of Statutory Instruments

PART 1

Assessments and Service Provision Determination

CHAPTER 1

COMMUNITY CARE ASSESSMENTS: AN OVERVIEW

1.1 Introduction

This book deals, primarily, with community care assessment and service provision decisions under the National Health Service and Community Care Act 1990 (the 1990 Act) after the new system introduced from 1 April 1993. It is directed both towards the way in which such decisions should be made, and the scope for challenge if they are reached unlawfully. The principal means of challenge will be by judicial review (see Chapter 8 and Appendix 5) but other forms of redress, including the statutory complaints machinery, will also be considered.

1.2 Community care

The philosophy of community care as expressed in the government White Paper *Caring for People* (Cmnd 849) 'means providing the right level of intervention and support to enable people to achieve maximum independence and control over their own lives'.

From 1 April 1993 when the relevant sections of the 1990 Act (most notably s 47) came into force, responsibility lies with local authorities for arranging community care for vulnerable groups, including the mentally ill.

The new system places financial control directly in the hands of the purchasing arms of social services departments across the country. It is the local authority's social services committee (see the Local Authority Social Services Act 1970, s 2, Sched 1) that will, as the resource holder, assess needs and make a decision on the nature of any community care services (as defined by s 46(3): see *below*) to be provided.

1.3 The assessment and service provision regime

The system for assessing need is contained in s 47 of the 1990 Act (see Appendix 1).

Section 47(1) places a general duty on a local authority, where it appears to that authority that any person for whom it may provide or arrange for the provision of community care services may be in need of any such services, to:

(a) carry out an assessment of his needs for those services (the assessment decision); and

(b) having regard to the results of such assessment then decide whether his needs call for the provision by it of any such services (the service provision decision).

The duties of assessing need and determining any service provision are, conceptually, separate although the decisions will, in practice, often be made together. It is important to note, however, that the factors affecting assessment of need do not necessarily dictate that an authority must decide to provide services commensurate with such need (see Chapters 2–4).

There is a qualification to the above duties which is set out in s 47(5) and (6) of the 1990 Act.

Where, in the opinion of the authority, the condition of a person is such that community care services are required as a matter of urgency then such services may be temporarily provided without carrying out a prior assessment of need (s 47(5)). However, as soon as practicable thereafter an assessment of needs is required to be made in accordance with the general s 47 regime, (s 47(6)).

There is no provision in the 1990 Act to suggest how s 47 assessments are to be carried out. However, s 47(4) provides that the Secretary of State may give directions as to the manner in which an assessment is to be carried out. In the absence of such directions (and as at 1 April 1993 no directions had been issued), the assessment 'shall be carried out in such manner and take such form as the local authority consider appropriate' (s 47(4)).

Services under the Chronically Sick and Disabled Persons Act 1970 fall outside the definition of community care services (see para 1.5 *below*). There is, nonetheless, a distinct assessment regime for need for such services which is contained in the Disabled Persons (Services, Consultation and Representation) Act 1986 and which will continue after 1 April 1993, (see ss 47(2), (7) and (8) of the 1990 Act). Whilst analytically extrinsic to the community care assessment regime, the assessment procedure for disabled persons may prove a helpful model of comparison for determining how some assessments should be conducted under the 1990 Act.

1.4 Complaints machinery

Section 50(1) of the 1990 Act inserts a new s 7B in the Local Authority Social Services Act 1970 (see Appendix 1). This enables the Secretary of State to order local authorities to establish a procedure for considering representations (including complaints) in relation to the discharge of, or any failure to discharge, any of their social services functions in respect of a 'qualifying individual'. By s 50(2), such an individual is defined as a person whom the authority has a power or duty to provide, or to secure the provision of, a service to him and whose need or possible need for such service has (by whatever means) come to the attention of the authority.

An order has been made, and directions given, requiring the establishment of a specific complaints procedure (see Chapter 7) with a rigid timetable for implementation. Often, though not invariably, an applicant disappointed by an assessment or service provision decision will be required to utilise an authority's complaints procedure prior to seeking judicial review. The legality and fairness of an authority's complaints regime is itself subject to judicial review.

1.5 Community care services

By s 46(3) of the 1990 Act (see Appendix 1) the expression 'community care services' is defined as services that a local authority may provide or arrange to be provided under any of the following provisions:

(1) Part III of the National Assistance Act 1948 (provision of accommodation and welfare services for blind, deaf, dumb, crippled and mentally disordered persons).

(2) Section 45 of the Health Services and Public Health Act 1968 (promotion of the welfare of old people).

(3) Section 21 of and Sched 8 to the National Health Service Act 1977 (care of mothers and young children, prevention, care and after-care, home-help and laundry facilities).

(4) Section 117 of the Mental Health Act 1983 (after-care for those persons who have ceased to be detained in hospital and then leave hospital).

The provision of home-helps under the 1977 Act and after-care services under s 117 are statutory duties rather than powers. Ostensibly, nothing in the 1990 Act operates to convert such duties to powers but the interrelationship between a duty to provide services and the discretionary service provision regime under the 1990 Act is not wholly clear (see para 4.3, where this aspect is analysed).

1.6 Directions and guidance

An authority's exercise of its social services functions in respect of assessment, service provision and complaints procedures is subject to guidance and directions issued by the Secretary of State.

Section 7 of the Local Authority Social Services Act 1970 provides that:

> Local authorities shall, in the exercise of their social services functions, including the exercise of any discretion ... act under the general guidance of the Secretary of State.

The phrase 'act under the general guidance' is to be contrasted with ss 7A, 7B and 7D of the 1970 Act, as inserted by s 50 of the 1990 Act, (see Appendix 1). These latter sections are concerned with directions given by the Secretary of State which:

(a) shall be given in writing (s 7A);
(b) may be given to a particular authority or class of authority or to authorities generally (s 7A);
(c) must be complied with by the authority (ss 7B(3), 7D(3)).

Although less than clearly expressed in the legislation, it is submitted that the distinction between guidance and directions is that the former must be taken into consideration by an authority when making assessment, service provision or complaints decisions. Where, however, guidance is sufficiently precise it has to be followed. Directions must, always, be strictly complied with.

No further formal content is prescribed by statute in respect of directions. However, in practice, directions made under ss 7B or 7D of the Local Authority Social Services Act 1970 specify their status and the section under which they are made in the document itself. Similarly guidance, whether in the form of circulars, letters or other documentation, is specific as to its status.

Guidance or directions issued by the Secretary of State which are unlawful are susceptible to judicial review (see, eg, *Laker Airways Ltd v Department of Trade* [1977] QB 643; *R v Secretary of State for Social Services, ex p Lewisham (etc) LBC* (1980) *The Times*, 26 February).

1.7   Core documents

The following documents (material parts of some of which are reproduced at Appendix 3) are particularly relevant to the processes of assessment, service provision and adjudication of complaints:

— The government White Paper *Caring for People*, Cmnd 849 ('the White Paper') (HMSO, 1989, ISBN 010 108492 7).
— *Community Care in the Next Decade and Beyond: Policy Guidance* ('Policy Guidance') (HMSO, 1990, ISBN 011 3213387).
— *Care Management and Assessment: Managers' Guide* ('Managers' Guide') (HMSO, 1991, ISBN 011 321464 2).
— *Care Management and Assessment: Practitioners' Guide* ('Practitioners' Guide') (HMSO, 1990, ISBN 011 321463 4).
— *Care Management and Assessment: Summary of Practice Guidance* ('Summary of Practice Guidance') (HMSO, 1991, ISBN 011 3214626).
— *Getting the Message Across: a Guide to Developing and Communicating Policies, Principles and Procedures on Assessment* ('Getting the Message Across') (HMSO, 1991, ISBN 011 321359 X).
— *The Right to Complain: Practice Guidance on Complaints Procedures in Social Services Departments* ('Right to Complain') (HMSO, 1991, ISBN 011 321434 0).

Important orders, circulars and directions (material parts of some of which are reproduced at Appendices 2 and 3), to date, are:

— Circular CI (92) 34 ('the Laming letter').
— Joint Circular on Housing and Community Care, Circular 10/92, LAC (92) 12 ('Housing and Community Care Circular').
— Local Authority Social Services (Complaints Procedure) Order 1990 (SI No 2244).
— National Assistance Act 1948 (Choice of Accommodation) Directions 1992, LAC (92) 27.
— Complaints Procedure Directions 1990 (Appendix to Policy Guidance).

1.8   Treatment

This book contains four parts designed to provide a systematic and practical approach to the community care legislation.

Part 1 deals with the following substantive questions relating to the processes of assessment and service provision:

7

(1) How should a local authority determine entitlement to assessment? (Chapter 2).

(2) How should the authority assess need? (Chapter 3).

(3) How should the authority determine service provision? (Chapter 4).

Part 2 covers procedural fairness in respect of:

(1) Assessment and service provision hearings (Chapter 5).

(2) Communication of assessment and service provision decisions (Chapter 6).

Part 3 is concerned with remedies in respect of a local authority's default in the exercise of its functions in relation to assessment and/or service provision and covers:

(1) Complaints procedures (Chapter 7).

(2) Judicial review (Chapter 8).

(3) The Secretary of State's default powers (Chapter 9).

(4) Private law actions for damages (Chapter 10).

Part 4 comprises Chapter 11 and deals with the financial aspect of assessment.

Finally, the Appendices contain statutory material and documentation relevant to assessment, service provision and complaints procedures in the form of guidance, orders, circulars and directions. They also include practical precedents including an imaginary judicial review case study, and specimen letters and decisions relating to the processes already considered.

CHAPTER 2

ENTITLEMENT TO ASSESSMENT

2.1 Criteria for entitlement

The condition for entitlement to assessment is a person's apparent need for the provision of community care services that a local authority is empowered to provide or arrange for that individual (s 47(1)(a) of the National Health Service and Community Care Act 1990). However, several questions arise from this ostensibly straightforward statement:

(1) What degree of need must be established so as to found a duty on the local authority to carry out an assessment?
(2) Must there be an application prior to any duty to assess?
(3) What degree of investigation is an authority required to undertake in order to determine entitlement to assessment?
(4) Will an authority be justified in refusing assessment where apparent need is only for those services which depend upon an individual's 'ordinary residence' in the authority's area or for services which the authority does not provide?

2.2 Apparent need

A careful reading of ss 47 and 50 of the 1990 Act (see Appendix 1) suggests that a person's apparent need for community care services is only required to be a 'possible' need. It does not have to appear to be an urgent or pressing or actual need (cf the similar considerations under the Housing Act 1985, s 62 and the Education Act 1981, s 5). Thus:

(1) The provision in s 47(1) of the 1990 Act makes assessment contingent merely upon the appearance to a local authority that a person 'may' be in need of particular community care services.

(2) This section also omits any requirement that such apparent need must be urgent.

(3) The definition of a 'qualifying person' in s 50 of the 1990 Act entitles a person, where the Secretary of State has established a complaints procedure (see Chapter 7), to make representations where:

    (i) the authority has a power or duty to provide such services for him; and

    (ii) his need or 'possible' need for such services has come to the authority's attention.

It would, clearly, be otiose to allow a person having merely a 'possible' need to embark on a complaints procedure if some higher threshold test were required for entitlement to assessment.

2.3 Must there be an application?

It is evident that no application is required to be made by or on behalf of a person needing community care services. The Policy Guidance states, at para 3.29 (see Appendix 3), that a carer may make application for assessment, but this is merely by way of clarification and does not introduce any restriction on the nature of the duty imposed upon the local authority.

Not only is there no express requirement for an application for assessment contained in the 1990 Act itself (cf, eg, the Housing Act 1985 homelessness regime), but it would run counter to:

(a) the fact that assessment must take place once the authority finds an appearance of need (s 47(1)(a) of the 1990 Act); and

(b) the fact that a person is entitled to invoke any designated complaints procedure if, *inter alia*, his need/possible need has, 'by whatever means', come to the attention of the authority. (See Appendix 1 for s 50 of the 1990 Act inserting s 7B into the Local Authority Social Services Act 1970.) This expression is, undoubtedly, wide enough to extend beyond a specific application.

2.4 Investigating entitlement to assessment

It is unclear whether a local authority may simply respond to situations where individual need is brought to its attention or whether there is some further obligation upon it to conduct investigations into potentially vulnerable groups so as to determine entitlement to assessment. The Laming letter (see

Appendix 3 at para 5) appears to assume the former without directly engaging the issue.

The fact that a complaints regime affords standing only to an individual whose need/possible need has 'come to the attention of the authority' (see s 50 of the 1990 Act and s 7B of the Local Authority Social Services Act 1970) does not immediately suggest that the authority is required to do more than act upon individual information received by it. If the position were otherwise, the right to invoke the complaints machinery would, presumably, be phrased more widely.

2.5   Refusal of assessment

Some community care services (eg ss 21 and 29 of the National Assistance Act 1948), are tied to the concept of 'ordinary residence'. Could an authority, therefore, decline to assess on the basis that, even were an assessment to be undertaken, there could be no resulting power or duty to provide such services because a particular applicant is not ordinarily resident in the authority's area?

The answer to this is to be found in the condition requiring assessment contained in the opening sentence of s 47(1) of the 1990 Act. Assessment is required only where it appears to the authority 'that any person for whom they may provide or arrange for the provision of community care services may be in need of any such services'.

Accordingly, the relevant criteria are not merely related to apparent need but also to the fact that a particular person is one for whom the authority is permitted to provide designated community care services in respect of those apparent needs.

The relevant test, therefore, is whether apparent need is shown for services which the authority may (rather than 'must') provide. If there is no power or duty to provide a particular service for which apparent need exists because an applicant is ordinarily resident in another local authority (or for any other reason) then the first local authority, asked to assess, may lawfully decline assessment.

A separate question is whether once assessment is undertaken, an authority must assess for services which it has decided not to provide. This is considered at para 3.2.

In the context of the 'ordinary residence' requirements, however, some caution is needed. As indicated, it is services which an authority 'may' provide or arrange to be provided that are relevant. Thus, for example, 'ordinary residence' may be dispensed with under certain provisions (s 24) of the

National Assistance Act 1948, and it is not always a necessary feature of the after-care duty under s 117 of the Mental Health Act 1983. If the authority may provide services independent of the 'ordinary residence' requirement, then it may not legitimately refuse to carry out an assessment of need for such services under the 1990 Act.

In determining whether an assessment may be validly refused it will always be important to identify the particular community care service in respect of which an apparent need is contended and the local authority's statutory powers in respect of such service.

2.6   Judicial review of a refusal to assess

Judicial review will be potentially available, (see though Chapter 8 at para 8.7), where a local authority acts unlawfully, irrationally or unfairly in refusing to carry out an assessment.

In principle, and having regard to the above discussion, it is suggested that judicial review is likely to arise where an authority:

(a) adopts an incorrect legal test as to the requisite degree of 'need' justifying assessment or an incorrect test as to the onus or standard of proof: given the wording of s 47(1) of the 1990 Act it is submitted that there cannot be any onus on an applicant to establish need or apparent need once the applicant's apparent need is brought to the authority's attention; or

(b) declines to make an assessment irrationally in the face of apparent need; or

(c) declines to make an assessment without investigation as to whether there is apparent need where such need is contended; or

(d) adopts an incorrect legal test as to its own power to provide or to arrange for the provision of particular community care services; or

(e) declines to make an assessment without affording any reasons for its decision (see *R v Civil Service Appeal Board, ex p Cunningham* [1991] 4 All ER 310, and the discussion at para 6.6).

On the other hand it is suggested that judicial review will not be available:

(a) merely because an authority does not pursue an investigation into the need of potentially vulnerable groups; and

(b) where an authority declines to assess because it has no statutory power or duty in respect of particular services for which apparent need exists.

CHAPTER 3

ASSESSING NEED

3.1 The duty to assess

Section 47(1)(a) of the National Health Service and Community Care Act 1990 imposes a duty on a local authority to carry out an assessment of a person's needs for the provision of community care services in circumstances where:

(a) that authority is empowered to provide or arrange for the provision of community care services for that person; and

(b) it appears to that authority that such person may be in need of any such services.

In analysing the scope of the assessment duty, once entitlement to assessment has been established (see Chapter 2), the following substantive issues arise:

(1) Is the authority required to assess need for community care services which it does not provide, even though statutorily empowered to do so?

(2) Is the authority required to assess need in circumstances where it cannot provide community care services which it is empowered to provide due to lack of resources?

(3) What enquiries must the authority make to determine need?

(4) Are the authority's duties affected in respect of disabled persons under s 47(2) of the 1990 Act?

(5) Are the authority's duties qualified in any way by the possible involvment of other authorities under s 47(3) of the 1990 Act?

(6) Is the duty to assess a continuing one or does it cease upon an assessment decision?

Questions of procedural fairness involving the manner in which assessments should be conducted, the speed with which decisions should be communicated and whether reasons must be provided are considered separately (see Chapters 5 and 6).

3.2 Assessing need for services not provided by the authority

It is clear that the assessment regime under the 1990 Act distinguishes between assessment and community care service provision since the duty to assess is set out separately in s 47(1)(a) of the Act whereas service provision is contained in s 47(1)(b) (see Appendix 1).

There is, in this respect, a direct comparison with the Education Act 1981, which envisages a division between the duty on a local education authority to assess special educational needs (s 5) and the duty to make a statement of such needs in circumstances where the authority is of the opinion that it should determine the special educational provision to be made (s 7).

Just as the 1981 Act does not impose a duty on an authority to make or to maintain a statement in respect of every child whose special educational needs are covered by the Act (see *R v Secretary of State for Education and Science and Another, ex p Lashford* [1988] 1 FLR 72), so too, the fact that a local authority has assessed a need for community care services that the authority is empowered to provide does not mean that the authority is required to provide them. (See Chapter 4 where the implications of this on service provision are considered.)

But if this is right it follows that the 1990 Act contemplates assessment as a service in its own right which can be distinguished from any services that are arranged in consequence (see Policy Guidance at para 3.15 and para 5 of the Laming letter).

The assessment service that is afforded by s 47(1)(a) is one of assessing need for community care services that an authority is empowered to provide for a particular person. Thus the authority must, whatever decision it arrives at in respect of service provision, investigate need for all services that an authority may provide for a particular individual rather than being limited to those community care services that are actually provided. A limiting of the assessment of need for which there were services that the authority had decided to make available would render such assessment amenable to judicial review.

Para 3.15 of the Policy Guidance suggests that an authority should, in assessing need, take into account the types of service that it has decided to make available. Para 2.20 of the Manager's Guide is in similar vein. It is submitted, however, that this approach would be unlawful if adopted at the assessment, as opposed to the service provision, stage.

The relevant extracts from the Policy Guidance, the Manager's Guide and the Laming Letter are reproduced at Appendix 3.

3.3 The effect of lack of resources on assessment of need

As indicated *above*, the authority's duty to assess need is free-standing from its duty to provide services. It is, therefore, immaterial to assessment that the authority does not have the resources to provide services in respect of which it assesses a need. The impact of lack of resources on service provision is considered at para 4.4.

As the Laming letter makes clear (see Appendix 3, para 13), there may be circumstances where an authority is entitled to take into account its available resources 'when deciding how to respond to an individual's assessment'. That is, however, quite different from taking resources into account when assessing need. The latter would be an error of law and potentially susceptible to judicial review.

3.4 General scope of enquiries

The legal scope of an authority's duty to enquire into a service user's need is to be distinguished from the type of procedure that an authority should follow. The latter issue is considered in Chapter 5. Failure to carry out adequate enquiry will render an authority's assessment amenable to judicial review subject to whether a particular applicant should, first, exhaust the complaints machinery (see Chapters 7 and 8).

Whilst the authority's duty may be affected by particular provisions of the 1990 Act (see paras 3.5 and 3.6 *below*), the general principles relating to such enquiries are likely to be similar to those developed under the Housing Act 1985 in respect of a local authority's duties to investigate issues of priority need and intentional homelessness.

Specifically (see Appendix 3 for the Laming letter, para 12), the assessment should focus on the difficulties which prompt individuals to seek assistance in the first place. It should take account of all the circumstances relevant to those individuals and, in particular, of:

(a) their capacities and incapacities;
(b) their preferences and aspirations;
(c) their living situation;
(d) the support available from relatives and friends; and
(e) any other sources of help.

In terms of principle, the minimum requirements that a court would place upon the scope of the duty to make a proper enquiry are as follows:

(1) Enquiries must cover all relevant factors (see: *R v Ryedale District Council, ex p Smith* (1983) 16 HLR 66).

(2) Users should be given the opportunity to explain their circumstances fully, and inconsistencies should be less readily relied upon where an applicant's native language is not English (see *R v Surrey Heath Borough Council, ex p Li* (1984) 16 HLR 79).

(3) Enquiries need not constitute 'CID-type' enquiries (see *Lally v Royal Borough of Kensington and Chelsea* (1980) *The Times*, 27 March), but the burden of making proper enquiry lies upon the authority rather than the applicant (see: *R v Reigate and Banstead Borough Council, ex p Paris* (1984) 17 HLR 103, *R v Gravesham Borough Council, ex p Winchester* (1986) 18 HLR 207).

(4) Where medical evidence is provided, the authority should either accept such evidence or make further enquiry: it should not reject such evidence without making such further enquiry (see *R v Bath City Council, ex p Sangermano* (1984) 17 HLR 94).

(5) Basic issues must be put to the user and an authority may not take into account that which the applicant failed to say but was not asked about (see *R v Wandsworth London Borough Council, ex p Rose* (1984) 11 HLR 107).

(6) An authority is entitled to rely on hearsay (see *R v Nottingham City Council, ex p Costello* (1989) *The Times*, 14 February).

3.5   Disabled persons

Section 47(2) of the 1990 Act provides that if at any time during a s 47 needs assessment it appears to the local authority that the applicant is a disabled person, then the authority shall proceed to make a decision as to the services that he requires under s 4 of the Disabled Persons (Services, Consultation and Representation) Act 1986 without his requesting it to do so under that section, and shall inform him that it will be doing so and of his rights under the 1986 Act.

The 1986 Act is concerned with the assessment of need for, and provision by an authority of, welfare services under s 2(1) of the Chronically Sick and Disabled Persons Act 1970. Such services are not 'community care services' under s 46(3) of the 1990 Act and, as such, fall outside the assessment regime contemplated by that Act.

It seems clear that a s 47 assessment is not necessarily the same as an assessment under the 1986 Act and that a full scale assessment under the 1986 Act must be offered to individuals appearing to the authority, using the s 47 assessment, to be disabled (see Appendix 3 for the Laming letter, para 9). In practice, however, where an individual is or appears to be disabled it is unlikely that assessment under the 1990 Act of need for community care services will be any less comprehensive than assessment under the 1986 Act (see para 5.1).

3.6   Other authorities

Section 47(3) of the 1990 Act provides that if at any time during a needs assessment under s 47 it appears to the authority that there may be a need for the provision to the applicant of services under the National Health Service Act 1977 (by a District Health Authority) or of any services under the Housing Act 1985 (by a local housing authority), the local authority shall notify the relevant authority and invite them to assist, to such extent as is reasonable in the circumstances, in the making of the assessment.

This is obviously important to those other authorities participating in the assessment process, given the further requirement of s 47(3) that the local authority undertaking the s 47 assessment must, in arriving at a service provision decision, take into account any services which are likely to be made available for the applicant by that authority.

The meaning of the phrase 'services which are likely to be made available' is unclear but it presumably represents a subjective evaluation on the part of the s 47 assessing authority of what services the District Health Authority or local housing authority are, following collaborative assessment under s 47, likely to provide to the applicant.

It is thus a *sine qua non* of the service provision decision, that should an ostensible need for the above-mentioned services emerge during the assessment, the District Health/local housing authority participate in the s 47 assessment provided that it is reasonable of the assessing authority to invite them to do so.

If either authority refuses unreasonably to participate it is open to the s 47 assessing authority to seek judicial review of such refusal. Indeed, unless the assessing authority does so it would face difficulty in reaching an informed service provision decision.

3.7 Reviewing assessment decisions

Clearly, there is scope for a local authority to review an assessment once made. Indeed, 'for frail people in the community, frequent reviews and adjustments of their care plans are likely to be needed' (see the Laming letter at para 31).

Such power is not expressly contained in the 1990 Act but it emerges from general principles of statutory interpretation that permit exercise of a statutory power from time to time unless contrary to the statutory intent (see s 12 of the Interpretation Act 1978).

Further, the requirement in s 47(1)(a) of the 1990 Act that an authority must assess an applicant's needs for community care services where there is an apparent need for such services, imposes a continuing duty to assess where the authority, notwithstanding an adverse first assessment, considers that there is such apparent need on reconsideration of the matter.

In many circumstances the need for review will arise from an alleged change of circumstances. Conceptually, however, this need not be the case and the care management philosophy attending the community care approach renders it unnecessary. If the authority is, for example, presented with new material or considers that it made a mistake of fact or law it would, undoubtedly, be entitled to review its previous assessment. This is a distinct power and does not require the complaints machinery to be invoked (see Chapter 7) by an applicant.

If a local authority unreasonably refuses to review its decision it would be susceptible to judicial review subject to a user's right (and possibly duty) to invoke the complaints machinery prior to seeking review (see Chapter 8 for full discussion). Provided that there is continuing need, a reassessment ought not to result in reduction or withdrawal of services even if service provision might be decided in a different way on reassessment (see the Laming letter at para 31 and Chapter 4).

Unreasonable reassessment may itself give rise to liability to judicial review or, more probably, to an applicant invoking the complaints procedure.

CHAPTER 4

SERVICE PROVISION

4.1 Scope of the duty

The separation of assessment of need from service provision has already been noted (see para 3.2).

Section 47(1)(b) of the National Health Service and Community Care Act 1990 provides that, following assessment of an individual, the local authority 'having regard to the results of that assessment, shall then decide whether his needs call for the provision by them' of particular services.

It seems clear that, after carrying out a needs assessment, an authority retains a discretion to determine the scope of its duty to provide services. This feature of discretion preceding duty is a familiar one and is replicated, for example, in ss 5 and 7 of the Education Act 1981 (special educational needs and local authority statements), and in ss 62–64 of the Housing Act 1985 (determination of matters giving rise to housing duties).

The following matters require particular analysis:

(a) the extent of the statutory discretion;

(b) the position in relation to community care services that are required to be provided;

(c) the relevance (if any) of lack of resources;

(d) the legality of a service provision policy;

(e) the extent to which service provision may be reviewed by the providing authority;

(f) the nature of the 'rights' created by a failure to determine service provision lawfully or provide services or to review service provision.

4.2 The statutory discretion to determine service provision

The principal aim of assessment is to arrive at a decision on whether services should be provided and in what form (see White Paper, para 3.2.12). Indeed, good practice dictates that communication of the assessment decision will normally involve not merely the results of assessment but also confirmation of an agreed care plan (see para 6.5).

It does not follow from this, however, that assessment of a particular need, as a matter of law, imposes a duty to provide services for which such need is established.

As has been seen (see para 3.2), there is a duty to assess need in respect of all community care services which a local authority is empowered or required to provide for a particular individual, in circumstances where an apparent need for such services comes to the attention of the authority (see s 47(1)(a) of the 1990 Act). But the fact that an authority is empowered to provide specific services does not mean that it must provide them as soon as need is established, since,were this so, a statutory power would automatically become equated with a duty.

The wording of s 47(1)(b) reinforces this view. It requires the authority to have regard to the results of the assessment. This means that the authority must take the assessment into account when deciding on its duty to provide community care services, but it does not have to pay 'slavish adherence' to such assessment, (see *De Falco v Crawley Borough Council* [1980] QB 460). It is entitled to exercise its discretion and take factors other than the assessment into account provided that it does so lawfully.

To be lawfully exercised, any discretion must be within the policy and objects of the relevant statute (*Padfield v Minister of Agriculture, Fisheries and Food* [1968] AC 997).

In the context of community care this inevitably means that the authority, in determining service provision, is (unless it is under a duty to provide services—see *below*), entitled to have regard to what is available and affordable.

In assessing availability the authority have a duty under s 47(3) of the 1990 Act to inform the relevant District Health Authority and/or housing authority if it considers that there is a need for provision by that authority in the light of the assessment, and to take into account any services likely to be made available by those authorities in reaching decisions on their own service provision.

Clearly, if a District Health Authority or housing authority unreasonably refuses to participate in the assessment it will not be possible to evaluate the nature of the services likely to be made available by that authority. In that event it may be that the local authority responsible for assessment/service provision should seek judicial review since, otherwise, an informed service provision decision will be incapable of being made.

Priority may legitimately be given to those whose needs are greatest (see White Paper, para 3.2.12; and the Laming letter, para 14). The extent of need is, clearly, at least in part dependent upon the support that is available from carers (see Policy Guidance, paras 3.27 *et seq.*) and from other authorities (see s 47(3) of the 1990 Act). Equally clearly, a local authority would err in law if it took into account the fact that a user or his family was able to meet the cost of service provision since such criterion is wholly unrelated to need. For this reason 'assessment of financial means should . . . follow the assessment of need and decisions about service provision' (see Policy Guidance, para 3.31).

In essence the authority has a responsibility to meet needs within the resources available. The Policy Guidance suggests that: 'The aim should be to secure the most cost-effective package of services that meets the user's care needs, taking account of the user's and carers' own preferences.' (See para 3.25.)

Consistent with the philosophy of community care, the Policy Guidance sets out a suggested order of preference of service provision (at para 3.24) towards the stated objective of preserving normal living as far as possible:

(1) Support for the user in his own home including day and domiciliary care, respite care, the provision of disability equipment and adaptations to accommodation as necessary.

(2) A move to more suitable accommodation, which might be sheltered or very sheltered housing, together with the provision of social services support.

(3) A move to another private household, ie to live with relatives or friends or as part of an adult fostering scheme.

(4) Residential care.

(5) Nursing home care.

(6) Long-stay care in hospital.

As in the case of assessments, the way in which a local authority exercises its discretionary power to determine the level of community care service provision must, being a social services function, be 'under the general guidance' of the Secretary of State (see s 7 of the Local Authority Social Services Act 1970), and 'in accordance with such directions as may be given' by the Secretary of State under s 7A of the 1970 Act as inserted by s 50 of the 1990 Act.

The legal issues associated with these provisions have already been outlined (see para 1.6). Essentially, the authority is required to take guidance into account and, where sufficiently precise, to follow it. It must, however, always act in accordance with any relevant directions issued. No directions have been issued in relation to service provision. Relevant extracts from the White Paper, the Laming Letter and the Policy Guidance are reproduced at Appendix 3 and the relevant sections of the 1990 Act and the Local Authority Social Services Act 1970 are reproduced at Appendix 1.

4.3   Mandatory community care services

Both the provision of home-helps under s 21 of the National Health Service Act 1977 and after-care services under s 117 of the Mental Health Act 1983, constitute statutory duties as opposed to powers.

The fact that these duties fall within the definition of 'community care services' under s 46(3) of the 1990 Act and, therefore, within the scope of the assessment regime under s 47 suggests, at first sight, that the provision of these services is included within the local authority's general discretion as to service provision under s 47(1)(b).

This cannot in fact be so since otherwise clear statutory duties would, merely by the creation of a framework for assessment of need, be converted to powers.

The correct construction of s 47(1)(b), in this context, is that where assessment of need discloses a need for services that are required to be provided, then the authority must determine that such need calls for the provision of those services.

The relevant sections of the 1990 Act are reproduced at Appendix 1.

4.4   Lack of resources

Traditionally, courts will not interfere in cases of discretionary allocation of resources (see, eg, *R v Hertfordshire County Council, ex p Three Rivers District Council* (1992) 90 LGR 526). In practical terms this means that a local authority is unlikely to be successfully judicially reviewed if it declines service provision in respect of community care services that it is empowered, but cannot afford, to provide (see Appendix 3 for the Laming letter, para 13).

However, the same considerations do not logically apply in circumstances where there is a statutory obligation to provide particular services (see para 4.3 *above*). Although there is a dearth of authority as to whether an authority can plead lack of resources in respect of a statutory duty it ought not, as a matter of principle, be allowed to do so since the requirement of the statute would thereby be subverted.

In *R v Ealing London Borough Council, ex p Leaman* ((1984) *The Times*, 10 February), Mann J was unimpressed by the local authority's argument that the statutory duty under s 2(1) of the Chronically Sick and Disabled Persons Act 1970 (not itself a 'community care service') must be read as being subject to the availability of resources. It is submitted that Mann J's approach is correct although, in the event, the authority abandoned the argument and no ruling was given.

4.5   Legality of a service provision policy

Decisions are often taken against a background of general policy. If the policy is lawful and is applied fairly, judicial review will be inappropriate.

It follows from the reasoning in para 4.3 *above* that any policy not to make service provision available for community care services that are mandatory would be unlawful and therefore subject to challenge in the courts.

A policy can be formulated legitimately in respect of discretionary service provision. However, such policy must not prevent consideration of 'all the issues which are relevant to each individual case as it comes up for decision' (see *Stringer v Minister of Housing and Local Government* [1970] 1 WLR 1281 at 1298, *per* Cooke J).

Sometimes, departure from a lawful policy may itself be unlawful. In *R v Home Secretary, ex p Ruddock* ([1987] 2 All ER 518), for example, Taylor J held that the Secretary of State was bound by a duty of fairness not to depart from published guidelines on the issuing of warrants for telephone tapping, albeit that the applicant was unaware of the terms of such guidelines. This is, in a sense, the converse of policy operating as a fetter on discretion and connotes that policy may occasionally act to circumscribe discretion, or at least to set limits to the extent to which discretion may be exercised without affording an opportunity to an applicant of making representations as to why existing policy ought not to be altered. (See also *R v Home Secretary, ex p Asif Khan* [1984] 1 WLR 1337.)

Given the statutory requirement for publication of community care plans under s 46(1) of the 1990 Act, and the fact that good practice dictates that authorities should produce accessible information as to departmental aims and priorities (see 'Getting the Message Across' at pp 10–11), there is a clear need for careful drafting of any relevant policy so as not to frustrate a user's legitimate expectation if a particular policy is departed from in an individual case.

4.6   Reviewing service provision

It is axiomatic that care needs for which services are being provided should be reviewed regularly by further assessment (see para 3.7; Appendix 3 for the Policy Guidance, para 3.51 and the Laming letter, para 31).

It is less clear that an authority has power in most circumstances to make a new determination as to the level of its service provision without a prior reassessment of need assuming that it is being contended that community care needs may have changed. The reason for this is that a determination as to service provision is contingent upon a decision as to need (see s 47(1) of the 1990 Act).

In practice, however, this is unlikely to prove a difficulty given that re-assessment may be extremely informal (see para 5.6) and that, in any event, the extent of service provision cannot be adequately determined without a knowledge of relevant need.

Even so, difficulties may arise where an authority's level of resources has risen so that it may now provide community care services for which a need was established on assessment but for which there were no previously available resources.

It is submitted that, in such circumstances, an authority may increase the level of its services without going through the reassessment process since, *ex hypothesi*, there is no point in the assessment process but circumstances do require the exercise of the power to determine increased provision (see s 12 of the Interpretation Act 1978). Furthermore, the language of s 47(1)(b) of the 1990 Act would appear to allow redetermination of service provision based upon the original assessment in circumstances where no new need was being contended.

Whether an authority could act to reduce the determined level of service provision, in the absence of a diminished need, is open to doubt. The cases on legitimate expectation referred to in para 4.5 *above* (*ex p Ruddock*; *ex p Khan*) suggest that the withdrawal of a benefit or advantage conferred as the result of an assurance or past practice will not be permitted by the courts unless the overwhelming public interest requires it and then only following representations. It follows that this is another area where a plea of lack of available resources may not assist the authority (see Appendix 3 for the Laming letter, para 31; and para 4.4 *above*).

4.7   Service provision and the courts

The issue here is the nature of the legal remedies theoretically available to a user in respect of:

(i)   the authority's failure to determine service provision lawfully or at all;
(ii) the authority's failure to review service provision lawfully or at all; and
(iii) the authority's failure to provide the requisite level of service having reached a determination that such level is required to be provided.

In *Cocks v Thanet District Council* ([1983] 2 AC 286), the House of Lords considered whether ss 4, 5 and 6 of the Housing (Homeless Persons) Act 1977 created any private law as opposed to public law rights. The leading speech was delivered by Lord Bridge who said (at 292):

> It is for the housing authority, once the duty to inquire has arisen, to make the appropriate inquiries and to decide whether they are satisfied, or not satisfied as the case may be, of the matters which will give rise to the limited housing duty or the full housing duty. These are essentially public law functions.

Lord Bridge contrasted this with the legal position once a decision had been reached. He observed (at 292–293):

> On the other hand, the housing authority are charged with executive functions. Once a decision has been reached by the housing authority which gives rise to the temporary, the limited or the full housing duty, rights and obligations are immediately created in the field of private law.

It has already been noted in para 4.1 *above* that the homelessness decision-making model is directly parallel to that of service provision. Applying the principles of the House of Lords in *Cocks* (see also *Mohram Ali v Tower Hamlets LBC* [1992] 3 WLR 208; *Tower Hamlets LBC v Abdi*, unreported, 16 September 1992; *Hackney LBC v Lambourne*, unreported, 27 November 1992), the following seems clear:

(1) The sole mode of legal challenge to a failure to determine service provision lawfully or at all is by way of judicial review since this is a decision-making function of the authority reached prior to any private law duty arising.

(2) For the same reason, judicial review is the only means of challenging a failure to review service provision lawfully or at all.

(3) Where a decision has been reached as to service provision, either initially or on review by the authority, such authority is then charged with the 'executive function' of implementation which is an obligation probably enforceable in private law including a claim for damages (see para 10.3).

Issues may arise, for example, as to whether judicial review may properly be sought before exhausting any available complaints machinery, or as to the scope of any potential damages claim in private law where service provision is withdrawn by virtue of an unlawful decision. These matters are separately considered in the chapters on remedies (see Chapters 8–10).

PART 2

Natural Justice in the Conduct and Communication of Assessment

CHAPTER 5

CONDUCTING THE ASSESSMENT

5.1 Fairness of assessment

This chapter is concerned with the fairness of the assessment process, (including any reassessment by way of review: see para 3.7). If an assessment is not conducted in accordance with the requirements of natural justice or procedural propriety it will, in principle, be susceptible to judicial review (see *Council of Civil Service Unions v Minister for the Civil Service* [1985] AC 374).

The National Health Service and Community Care Act 1990 is largely silent as to how an assessment should be carried out. This does not mean, however, that natural justice is irrelevant. As Byles J observed in *Cooper v Wandsworth Board of Works* ((1863) 14 CB(NS) 180 at 194:

> A long course of decisions . . . establish, that although there are no positive words in a statute requiring that the party shall be heard, yet the justice of the common law will supply the omission of the legislature.

Where it is clear that additional steps are needed to achieve justice and will not frustrate the apparent purpose of the legislation the court will readily imply them into the Act (see, eg *per* Lord Reid in *Wiseman v Borneman* [1971] AC 297 at 308).

There are, in any event, three statutory provisions that provide additional underpinning for the implication of natural justice into the assessment process.

As has been seen, ss 7 and 7A of the Local Authority Social Services Act 1970 require a local authority, exercising social services functions, to act (respectively) 'under' guidance of the Secretary of State or 'in accordance with' directions issued by the Secretary of State. A large amount of guidance has already been given, (see, eg Appendix 3) and this is clearly designed to ensure fairness in the undertaking of authorities' assessment procedures. This guidance must be taken account of when conducting assessments and followed in spirit if not to the letter (see para 1.6, where the legal effect of guidance is considered).

Secondly, s 47(4) of the 1990 Act provides for the giving of directions by the Secretary of State as to the manner in which an assessment is to be carried out. In the absence of such directions (none have yet been given) the assessment 'shall be carried out in such manner and take such form as the local authority consider appropriate'. This discretion must, be exercised in such a way as to achieve fairness in the assessment process in order to fall within the policy and objects of the Act (*Padfield v Minister of Agriculture, Fisheries and Food* [1968] AC 997).

Finally, s 47(7) of the 1990 Act provides that s 47 is without prejudice to s 3 of the Disabled Persons (Services, Consultation and Representation) Act 1986. Given that the 1986 Act lays down specific criteria of fairness with regard to assessments for disabled persons in respect of services under s 2 of the Chronically Sick and Disabled Persons Act 1970 (see *below*), and given that a local authority will frequently be conducting assessments concurrently under the 1986 and 1990 Acts (see s 47(2) of the 1990 Act and para 3.5), it is improbable that a different form of assessment is intended to be carried out according to whether a disabled person is seeking to establish a need for services under the 1970 or 1990 Act. But if that is right it must follow that the standard of assessment contained in s 3 of the 1986 Act provides a model for how assessments should be undertaken for all persons under the 1990 Act. Because of the wide range of possible assessments, however, s 3 is particularly helpful as a comparative model where a comprehensive assessment is required (see *below*).

5.2 Scope of natural justice in the assessment procedure

It is sometimes said that natural justice has twin pillars supporting it: (i) the rule against bias; and (ii) the right to be heard (see *Kanda v Government of Malaya* [1962] AC 322 at 337).

In the context of community care service assessment, however, the particular aspects of fairness likely to be relevant are:

(a) legitimate expectation; and
(b) the right to be heard.

Legitimate expectation will be relevant where a local authority has (as it should, see Appendix 3 for the Laming letter, paras 10 and 11) published criteria as to its assessment procedures/criteria for eligibility, or has developed a practice of conducting assessments, and then seeks to depart from such criteria or practice (see para 5.3, *below*).

Procedural fairness, in allowing a user to put his case as to need, embraces a number of aspects. In *Ridge v Baldwin* ([1964] AC 40 at 65) Lord Reid emphasised that the appropriate test for ensuring that a person has had the opportunity of putting his case was what a reasonable man would consider to be fair in the particular circumstances. This general statement of principle requires scrutiny of several different stages of the assessment process (see paras 5.4–5.6, *below*).

5.3   Legitimate expectation

The notion of 'legitimate expectation' has greatly extended the boundaries of natural justice to the point where it can be said to resemble a requirement of administrative fairness in a wide range of situations.

As formulated by Lord Diplock in *Council of Civil Service Unions v Minister for the Civil Service* ([1985] AC 374), legitimate expectation affords a form of protection against adverse decisions inconsistent with some benefit or advantage where the decision-maker has conferred such benefit or advantage as a result of past practice or assurance. As stated by Lord Diplock, and in most of the case law since, the concept has, primarily, been applied in a procedural manner so as to ensure that no such adverse decision will be taken without first giving the affected party an opportunity of making representations as to why the particular benefit/advantage should not be withdrawn.

It would, nonetheless, be unwise to view legitimate expectation as a solely procedural concept. Two modern decisions—*R v Home Secretary, ex p Asif Khan* [1984] 1 WLR 1337 and *R v Home Secretary, ex p Ruddock* [1987] 1 WLR 1482—show that the doctrine comes close to permitting the conferment of a substantive benefit as opposed merely to a right to make representations. In *Khan*, Parker LJ went so far as to suggest that a new policy could only be adopted against the recipient of a circular after considering whether the overriding public interest demanded it.

Local authorities are advised to publish, in accessible form, information about their care services, including authorities' criteria for determining when services should be provided and the assessment procedures showing how and where to apply for an assessment, and giving information about how to make representations and complaints (see Appendix 3 for the Policy Guidance, para 3.18).

It seems likely that if a local authority were to depart from published criteria (or from past practice) as to either its manner of conducting assessments or for assessing need, without at least affording a user the opportunity of making representations and, perhaps also, without considering whether the wider public interest required such departure, it would render itself susceptible to judicial review. In *Khan*, the Secretary of State was held by a majority of the Court of Appeal to be bound by a circular limiting the ambit of his discretion to turn down an application for entry clearance for a child. Exactly the same principle appears to be relevant to an authority's published information upon which a user or his representatives rely.

5.4   Pre-assessment considerations

All the guidance issued emphasises the importance of local authorities presenting clear and accessible published information about their assessment practices in a form that reaches users (see also para 5.3 *above*). This is consistent with the importance that natural justice accords to a person being given notice of a hearing so as to be able to put his case properly (see *R v Thames Magistrates' Court, ex p Polemis* [1974] 1 WLR 1371).

According to the Managers' Guide (see Appendix 3, para 2.5) such information should, as a matter of good practice, include:

(a)   the range of needs for which the agency accepts responsibility;

(b)   the aims, priorities and objectives of the agency;

(c)   the types of services available from all sectors and the needs for which they cater;

(d)   the criteria determining access to resources;

(e)   the referral, assessment and review procedures within and between agencies;

(f)   the entitlements of users and carers to information, participation and representation, including provision for equal opportunities;

(g)   the charging policies;

(h)   the standards by which the agency will monitor its performance, including response times to referrals;

(i)   complaints and feedback procedures.

Failure to provide information in sufficiently clear form could, itself, form a ground of challenge in judicial review proceedings.

5.5   Participants in assessment process

The individual service user and normally (with his or her agreement) any carers, should, so far as possible, be involved throughout an assessment (see Appendix 3 for the Policy Guidance, para 3.15). This follows from the statutory scheme of assessment which is to determine individual need for community care services. Additionally, natural justice may require that a service user be permitted the use of a representative to put his case for him if desired (cf *R v Leicester City JJ, ex p Barrow* [1991] 3 WLR 368). Failure to permit a user, carer or representative access to the assessment procedure would render an authority, *prima facie*, amenable to judicial review.

There may be circumstances where the assessment is so straightforward that it involves only minimum participation by the user or someone acting on his behalf (see para 5.6, *below*). More likely to arise, however, is the situation where a user either does not want to or is unable to participate actively.

Clearly, a user cannot be forced to participate in an assessment against his will. A local authority is, nonetheless, under a duty to make an assessment in any case where apparent need for community care services capable of being provided by the authority is brought to its attention (see Appendix 1 for s 47(1) of the 1990 Act).

Thus, in circumstances where the user is unwilling to participate in an assessment, such assessment must take place on the basis of the information brought before the authority by the carer or other third party or on the basis of information that it would otherwise seek on assessment. If the carer does not wish to participate it is unlikely that he may, thereafter, complain as to a breach of natural justice by the authority by reason of his not having made representations (see, eg, *R v Nailsworth Licensing JJ, ex p Bird* [1953] 1 WLR 1046).

The position is slightly different where a user is unable to participate actively. The Policy Guidance (see Appendix 3 at para 3.16) indicates in general terms that in such circumstances 'it is even more important that he or she should be helped to understand what is involved and the intended outcome'.

This does not, however, deal with the overall problem of procedural fairness. Section 3(6) of the Disabled Persons (Services, Consultation and Representation) Act 1986 requires an authority, during an assessment under that Act, to provide such services as in its view are necessary to ensure that any mental or physical incapacity does not prevent the making of representations by or on behalf of a disabled person.

As a matter of principle it would seem that similar assistance should be given, where appropriate, for the purpose of an assessment under the 1990

Act. Indeed, s 47(5) and (6) of the 1990 Act provide some support for this view empowering, as they do, the provision of community care services without assessment where the condition of a service user is such that, in the authority's view, he requires such services as a matter of urgency.

Given the statutory context it is submitted that an authority should, in all but the simplest case, permit oral representations to be made by a user or his representative.

Participants in assessment from the authority's perspective are considered *below*.

5.6 The assessment

It is clear that every assessment must be handled on its merits. Arrangements should normally include an initial screening process to determine the appropriate form of assessment (see Appendix 3 for the Policy Guidance, para 3.20; and the Laming letter, para 10).

Some people may only require advice and assistance without formal assessment. In other cases assessment may, in practice, already have taken place as where, for example, a patient has already been assessed for discharge from hospital. In the latter case, subject to the user wishing to make further representations, the prior assessment will probably form the basis of the assessment decision (see Appendix 3 for the White Paper, para 3.2.11; also the Policy Guidance, paras 3.41–3.45).

Other cases will inevitably be more complex and require more elaborate procedures. Such procedures 'should be sufficiently comprehensive and flexible to cope with all levels and types of need presented by different client groups' (see Appendix 3 for the Policy Guidance, para 3.20).

The Managers' Guide contains a table (reproduced in Appendix 3), containing a model for six possible types of assessment according to the type of need and the services to be considered and giving an indication of the type of staff, number of agencies involved and an example of a service outcome.

Where an apparent need is simple and defined the simplest type of assessment carried out by reception or administrative staff is likely to be sufficient. At the top end of the scale a comprehensive assessment will be required for ill-defined, high risk and severe need and this should be carried out by professionally qualified and/or specialist professional staff on a multiple agency basis. In all assessments GPs ought generally, as a matter of good practice, to be consulted (see Appendix 3 for the Policy Guidance, paras 3.47–3.48; and the Laming letter, para 9).

In all cases where a local authority, in assessing need, proposes to act on the basis of information not available to the user, such information must be disclosed to the user or his representative and failure to do so is a breach of natural justice (see *Mahon v Air New Zealand* [1984] AC 808; *R v Mental Health Review Tribunal, ex p Clatworthy* [1985] 3 All ER 699). A related consideration, underpinned by statute, is that confidential health and personal social services information on a service user should not be disclosed to other agencies for the purpose of assessment without obtaining the user's written consent to such disclosure (see Appendix 3 for the Policy Guidance, para 3.50).

CHAPTER 6

COMMUNICATION OF DECISIONS

6.1 Introduction

The National Health Service and Community Care Act 1990 is silent as to the form or timing of assessment and service provision decisions. In this chapter the following particular problems are addressed:

(1) Given that assessment and service provision determination are separate processes (see para 3.2) must decisions in respect of each be delivered separately?
(2) Must such decision(s) be in writing?
(3) What is the minimum content of each decision?
(4) Do reasons have to be provided?
(5) Within what timescale must such decision(s) be given?
(6) To whom should such decisions be communicated?

6.2 Separate decisions

Although assessment is, conceptually, separate from service provision determination, the only 'decision' that a local authority is statutorily required to come to is one on whether it should provide community care services (see Appendix 1 for s 47(1)(b) of the 1990 Act). The assessment process is a necessary constituent of such a decision because the authority must make its decision 'having regard to the results of the assessment'.

Thus, whilst it is clear that assessment means that the authority will have to 'decide' on a particular applicant's needs for community care services under s 47(1)(a) of the 1990 Act, it is apparent that the authority's 'decision' is necessarily contained in the service provision determination itself. The authority makes a single decision but it contains separate constitutive elements.

In many cases, however, a service user will be entitled to sight of his assessment under regulations made pursuant to the Access to Personal Files Act 1987. (See reg 2(1) of the Access to Personal Files (Social Services) Regulations 1989 (SI 1989 No 206) subject to possible exemption under reg 8.)

6.3   Decision in writing

Nothing in the 1990 Act expressly requires that the authority's assessment or service provision determinations must be recorded in writing.

It is submitted that there is no such universal requirement; if it were otherwise, an unnecessary burden would be placed upon local authorities habitually conducting informal assessments and making service provision decisions of a straightforward nature.

This view is supported by the Manager's Guide (para 2.24) which observes that decisions 'in respect of simple needs' may be communicated 'on a verbal basis'. However, given the probable requirement that most assessment/ service provision decisions provide reasons (see *below*), it is likely that the courts would require written decisions in relation to anything other than an ostensibly straightforward case. The Manager's Guide and Policy Guidance (see respectively, para 2.24 and para 3.27) indicate that a written decision should be given where an assessment results in the offer of a continuing service. However, whilst this is technically correct, it is almost certainly not exclusive of the situations where an authority's decision should be given in writing. Certainly, a decision in writing should always be supplied on request (Policy Guidance, para 3.27).

The relevant extracts from the Manager's Guide and the Policy Guidance are reproduced at Appendix 3.

6.4   Content of assessment decision

The objective of assessment is to determine individual need for community care services that a local authority is empowered to provide or arrange for the provision of (see Appendix 1 for s 47(1)(a) of the 1990 Act).

Thus, an authority's assessment should define an individual's specific needs in relation to identified community care services irrespective of whether the authority has decided to provide such services. A useful definition of 'need' in this context is 'the requirement of individuals to enable them to achieve, maintain or restore an acceptable level of social independence or quality of life' (see Summary of Practice Guidance, para 11).

The assessment should, it is submitted, be reasoned (see *below*). On that basis the assessment should explain, intelligibly, the material upon which it has determined need. If there is material before it, or representations made, which the authority has rejected the basis for such rejection should be clearly set out. From a practical perspective the assessment should be clearly demarcated in the decision and separated from the service provision element of the reasoning.

6.5 Content of service provision decision

Section 47(1)(b) of the 1990 Act requires a service provision decision to be made (having regard to the authority's assessment) about whether the applicant's needs call for provision by the authority of any service for which need is established. The criteria affecting such decision have already been considered (see Chapter 4).

The content of a decision as to service provision connotes the following:

(1) Determination of the issue of whether the applicant's needs (as recorded in the assessment) call for the provision by the authority for particular services and, if so, what services.

(2) The reasons for that decision including identification of the material relied upon by the authority in arriving at such decision (see *below*) and indicating why, if it be the case, that material before it, or representations made, were rejected.

(3) Reference to the existence of a complaints procedure (see Policy Guidance at para 6.29).

In practice, once needs have been assessed any decision to provide particular community care services or arrange for the provision of such services should (if possible) be set out in the form of a care plan (see Policy Guidance, para 3.24). The plan should make clear the extent to which an individual's needs qualify for assistance under the authority's eligibility criteria for services (see Laming letter, para 15).

The Policy Guidance (at para 3.24) suggests that a care plan should be agreed. 'Care planning' is defined in Appendix B of the Guidance as:

the process of negotiation between assessor, applicant, carers and other relevant agencies on the most appropriate ways of meeting assessed needs within available resources and incorporating them into an individual care plan.

If agreement is not possible the points of difference should be recorded, (Policy Guidance at para 3.25).

The decision should (see Policy Guidance, para 3.26 and the Laming letter, para 15) include agreement as to what is to be done, by whom and by when, with clearly identified points of access to each of the relevant agencies for the service user, carers and for the service manager.

The relevant extracts from the 1990 Act, the Policy Guidance and the Laming letter are reproduced at Appendices 1 and 3.

6.6   Reasons

R v Civil Service Appeal Board, ex p Cunningham ([1991] 4 All ER 310) establishes that: (i) there is, except as laid down by statute, no general duty in English law to give reasons for a decision; but that (ii) natural justice may, in appropriate circumstances, require the giving of reasons. The regulating principle is that:

> Unless the citizen can discover the reasoning behind the decision, he may be unable to tell whether it is reviewable or not and so he may be deprived of the protection of the law. A right to reasons is therefore an indispensable part of a sound system of judicial review. (See Wade, *Administrative Law*, (Oxford University Press) 6th edn 1988, pp 547–548).

This was the reasoning of the majority of the Court of Appeal in *Cunningham*. Lord Donaldson of Lymington MR, who gave the leading judgment in that case, ended his decision with the words:

> I would therefore dismiss the appeal not only upon the ground of legitimate expectation . . . but also upon the broader ground that fairness requires a tribunal such as the board to give sufficient reasons for its decision to enable the parties to know the issues to which it addressed its mind and that it acted lawfully.

McCowan LJ, in reaching the same conclusion, stated:

> I am influenced by the following factors:
> (1) There is no appeal from the board's determination of the amount of compensation.
> (2) In making that determination the board is carrying out a judicial function.
> (3) The board is susceptible to judicial review.

(4) The procedure provided for by the code, that is to say the provision of a recommendation without reasons, is insufficient to achieve justice.

(5) There is no statute which requires the courts to tolerate that unfairness.

(6) The giving of short reasons would not frustrate the apparent purpose of the code.

(7) It is not a case where the giving of reasons would be harmful to the public interest.

These considerations drive me to the view that this is a case where the board should have given reasons . . .

In essence, therefore, where a 'fully judicial body' (*per* Lord Donaldson MR at p 318j), susceptible to judicial review and from which there is no right of appeal, gives a decision in a case where to give reasons would prejudice neither the purpose of the material statute nor the public interest, that body ought to give reasons for its decision, so that the individual affected thereby may know whether the decision was made lawfully.

If, as in *Cunningham*, the Civil Service Appeal Board is performing a 'fully judicial function' in quantifying compensation for unfair dismissal then it is difficult to resist the conclusion that a local authority making assessment and service provision decisons is performing an equivalent function. Assuming that to be right, such authority must (independent of policy guidance) provide reasons for its decisions. Reasons must be 'adequate and intelligible' (see *Re Poyser and Mills Arbitration* [1964] 2 QB 467).

Failure to provide such reasons may lead to judicial review although if lack of reasons is the sole substantive ground for review the court may simply order the authority to provide reasons rather than quash the decision itself.

6.7 Time within which decisions must be reached

No express time limits are laid down in the 1990 Act for the communication of assessment or service provision decisions. Nonetheless such decisions should be made on a timely basis (see Appendix 3 for the White Paper, para 3.2.11).

Unreasonable delay in determination of assessment or service provision may lead to judicial review. In *R v Secretary of State for the Home Department, ex p Phansopkar* ([1976] QB 606), for example, mandamus was granted requiring the Home Secretary to determine applications for certificates proving a right of abode in a reasonable time.

What constitutes unreasonable delay in the context of community care assessments is a matter of fact and degree. Probably such delay must be unreasonable in the sense that no reasonable local authority could have delayed for such a period (see *R v IRC, ex p Opman International UK* [1986] 1 WLR 568; *R v Secretary of State for the Home Department, ex p Rofathullah* [1989] QB 219). The courts are traditionally reluctant to interfere in the context of the time within which a public body should perform its functions and deploy its resources (see *Rofathullah, per* Purchas LJ).

6.8 Recipient of decisions

The service user and carer must, clearly, be provided with the assessment/service provision decision. With the user's permission assessment information should be passed on to those responsible for care delivery (see Appendix 3 for the Policy Guidance, para 3.26).

PART 3

Legal Remedies

CHAPTER 7

COMPLAINTS PROCEDURES

7.1 Legal source of complaints procedures

Section 7B of the Local Authority Social Services Act 1970 (as inserted by s 50 of the National Health Service and Community Care Act 1990) creates machinery for a complaints procedure to be set up where a local authority has improperly discharged, or failed to discharge, any of its social services functions. The term 'social services functions' is, clearly, wide enough to embrace, and does embrace, assessments or service provision decisions.

By s 7B(1) the Secretary of State is empowered by order to require local authorities to establish a procedure for considering any representations (including any complaints) made to them by a 'qualifying individual' or anyone acting on his behalf in relation to the discharge of, or failure to discharge, any of an authority's social services functions in respect of that individual. The Local Authority Social Services (Complaints Procedure) Order 1990 (SI No 2244) provides, somewhat repetitively, that:

> Every local authority shall establish a procedure for considering any representations (including any complaints) which are made to them by a qualifying individual, or anyone acting on his behalf, in relation to the discharge of, or any failure to discharge, any of their social services functions in respect of that individual.

A person is a 'qualifying individual', under s 7B(2), if:

(a) the authority has a power or a duty to provide, or to secure the provision of, a service for him; and

(b) his need or possible need for such a service has (by whatever means) come to the authority's attention.

Local authorities are bound by s 7B(3) to comply with any directions of the Secretary of State as to the procedure to be adopted in considering representations, and as to the taking of any necessary action in consequence thereof. They must also give such publicity to their procedures as they consider appropriate (see s 7B(4)).

The Secretary of State has issued directions as to the creation of complaints procedures by virtue of the Complaints Procedure Directions 1990 (reproduced at Appendix 2). In addition, helpful practice guidance is contained in the Policy Guidance and in the Right to Complain. This guidance must be taken into account by an authority in so far as the guidance is not reproduced in the directions (see s 7 of the 1970 Act and para 1.6).

The Policy Guidance also states (see Appendix 3, para 6.9) that such guidance is not exhaustive and that in formulating or revising its complaints procedures an authority may find it helpful to refer, for example, to the code of practice on complaints procedures issued by the Local Authority Associations and the Commission for Local Administration in 1978, and to the booklet— 'Open to Complaints: guidelines for social services complaints procedures'— published by the National Consumer Council (with the National Institute for Social Work) in 1988.

Given that complaints in respect of an authority's failure to perform its social services functions are required to be considered under a specific complaints regime, a user will need to consider carefully whether such procedure (or specific stage of the procedure) constitutes an alternative remedy so as to preclude judicial review of an assessment or service provision decision before the procedure is exhausted. This issue is considered in detail in Chapter 8, and the observations made in respect of susceptibility to judicial review in this chapter must be read as being subject to that issue.

7.2   Publicising the complaints regime

Although publicity for an authority's complaints procedures is left to the authority's discretion (see s 7B(4) of the Local Authority Social Services Act 1970), the Policy Guidance (see Appendix 3, para 6.26) suggests three potential methods:

(1) Leaflets explaining the procedure in simple terms and referring to the role of the Local Government Ombudsman and to the separate leaflet 'Complaint about the Council?'. The leaflet should also give the name, address and telephone number of the person responsible for administering the procedure and be widely accessible to all including ethnic minorities and blind people.

(2) Notices displayed in the authority's offices.

(3) Visual and oral presentations.

In addition, an assessment or service provision decision should itself contain reference to the authority's complaints procedure (see para 6.5, and Appendix 3 for the Policy Guidance, para 6.29).

Failure to publicise an authority's complaints procedure so as to deny a user any effective opportunity of having his complaint heard would be susceptible to judicial review either as a breach of the authority's discretion under s 7B(4) of the Local Authority Social Services Act 1970 (see *Padfield v Minister of Agriculture Fisheries and Food* [1968] AC 997) or, more simply, as a violation of natural justice.

By contrast, if an authority has given full publicity to its complaints procedure, then if such published procedures were to be departed from a user or those acting on his behalf should be given 'full and serious consideration whether there is some overriding public interest' justifying such departure (see *R v Home Secretary, ex p Asif Khan* [1984] 1 WLR 1337). Failure to do so could give rise to a challenge to any substitute procedure as a breach of the user's legitimate expectation. However, if the procedure adopted is fair and does not lead to injustice then, even if there is variation from the authority's published procedures, an application for judicial review would be unlikely to succeed given that 'the so-called rules of natural justice are not engraved on tablets of stone' (see *Lloyd v McMahon* [1987] AC 625 at 702), and that the procedure ought not to be operated inflexibly (see para 7.3 *below*). Ideally, however, an authority's published procedures should state clearly that departure from stages of the procedure may be necessary according to the circumstances of the individual case.

7.3   Stages of the procedure

There are three stages to an authority's complaints procedure:

— the informal or problem-solving stage;
— the formal or registration stage; and
— the review stage.

By Direction 4(1) of the 1990 Directions the local authority must appoint one of its officers to assist the authority in the co-ordination of all these stages of its consideration of a complaint. The authority must also ensure that all members or officers involved in the handling of complaints are familiar with the procedures contained in the Directions (see Appendix 2, Direction 4(2)).

Nothing in an authority's complaints regime is intended to affect other potential avenues of complaint, such as the right of a user to approach a local councillor, or to complain (if appropriate) to the Mental Health Act Commission (see Appendix 3 for the Policy Guidance, paras 6.34 and 6.35). An authority may lawfully refuse access to its complaints procedure in respect of anonymous complaints or complaints of a general nature unconnected with the performance of the authority's social services functions (see Appendix 3 for the Policy Guidance, para 6.5).

However, it is not open to an authority to refuse access to its complaints machinery on the basis that an alternative complementary method of recourse is available to a user since this would constitute unlawful delegation of power (see *Barnard v National Dock Labour Board* [1953] 2 QB 18), as well as falling foul of the authority's express statutory obligation to maintain a complaints procedure.

7.4   The informal stage

Direction 5(1) of the Complaints Procedure Directions 1990 provides that where a local authority receives representations from a qualifying individual (see para 7.1 *above*) it should first attempt to resolve the matter informally.

There are a number of points to be made as to the implementation of this preliminary stage of the complaints procedure:

(1) The fact that this stage is categorised as 'informal' does not mean that it is 'casual' (see Right to Complain, para 4.3). Its purpose is to solve problems at the earliest possible stage and pursuing every case to the final stage would undermine this concept (Right to Complain at para 4.8). Representations may, at this stage, be oral (see Policy Guidance at para 6.17). Although the 1990 Directions are not entirely clear on this point it seems that informal representations need not be recorded under Direction 9 since the recording of representations appears to constitute the registration stage and the commencement of formal time limits, (see *below*).

(2) The informal stage should not, however, be used as a device to prevent or dissuade users from making a formal complaint (Right to Complain, para 4.5). Procedure operated in this way would be liable to challenge on judicial review as being void for improper motives (see *Wheeler v Leicester City Council* [1985] AC 1054).

(3) However, disregard of this stage by an authority may be justified in appropriate circumstances (see Policy Guidance, para 6.30). This reflects the principle that inflexible application of a procedure in the

name of fairness may itself produce unfairness (here delay) and, therefore, be unlawful (see *R v Police Complaints Board, ex p Madden* [1983] 1 WLR 447). For example, serious allegations may require the involvement of senior staff at an early stage and a more formal process (Policy Guidance, para 6.30). Certainly, if a complainant wishes to go straight to the formal stage of the procedure he should be helped to do so (Right to Complain, para 4.9).

(4) For similar reasons, different procedures from the conventional complaints regime may need to be utilised. The Policy Guidance (para 6.30) suggests that where allegations indicate the commission of a criminal offence, and such allegations are serious and substantial, the police should be informed immediately and local procedures contained in an authority's standing orders should be followed.

(5) Procedures for reviewing assessment and service provision decisions (see para 3.7) may overlap, to some extent, with the informal (or even registration) stage of the complaints procedure. It may be that a complaint is really a request for reconsideration of the assessment. Any review of an assessment decision should make reference to how a complaint may be pursued further (see Policy Guidance, para 6.29). Further, at the registration stage a complaint about a particular decision will be referred to the original decision-maker to see and take action on it (Right to Complain, para 4.13).

(6) Although the 1990 Directions do not appear to require an authority to provide support for complainants at the informal stage, the Policy Guidance (para 6.28), makes it clear that such support and encouragement should be available at the earliest stage since by providing it 'the chances of resolving the matter there and then increase'.

(The relevant extracts from the Complaints Procedure Directions 1990, the Right to Complain and the Policy Guidance are reproduced at Appendices 2 and 3.)

7.5   The registration stage

Direction 5(2) of the 1990 Directions stipulates that if the matter cannot be resolved to the complainant's satisfaction, the local authority must give or send to him an explanation of the registration and review stages of the complaints procedure (as set out in the Directions) and ask him to submit a written representation if he desires to proceed.

The requirement that a complainant be sent or given an explanation of the procedure set out in the Directions is strict and is likely to be regarded as mandatory so that it will be serious to disregard it (see, eg *Grunwick Processing Laboratories Ltd v ACAS* [1978] AC 655). This requirement differs from the general exhortation to authorities to publish their complaints procedures (see *above*), since it is not the authority's particular procedure but, rather, the procedure contained in the 1990 Directions that must be provided. Additionally, the information must be provided directly to the complainant as opposed to being published generally.

It is at this stage that the authority is, by Direction 5(3), required to offer assistance and guidance to the complainant on the use of the complaints procedure or, at least, to provide advice as to where the complainant may obtain such advice and guidance.

Those providing such support must ensure that a complainant's representations reflect what the complainant wishes to say and should ask the complainant to sign it (see Appendix 3 for Right to Complain, para 4.10).

Whilst there may be technical arguments open to a local authority that it cannot be held to have acted unlawfully in respect of inadequate representations upon which a third party, rather than the authority, has advised, the general duty to act fairly probably requires the authority to ensure that there is no ambiguity in the representations presented to it. In particular, the term 'representations' has a specific meaning under Direction 2(1) of the 1990 Directions and means representations (including complaints) referred to in s 7B(1) of the Local Authority Social Services Act 1970. Section 7B(1) necessitates that representations must be 'in relation to the discharge of, or any failure to discharge' any social services functions of the authority in respect of the complainant.

The next stages of the registration stage may be summarised thus:

(1) Every representation received must be registered (Direction 9). This does not preclude an oral hearing but it seems clear that the registration stage is envisaged, primarily, as a formal written record of complaint and response thereto.

(2) Such registered complaint must be considered and responded to within 28 days of the authority receiving the complaint. If this is not possible an explanation of the position must be provided to the complainant within the first 28 days including the reason why it is not possible and an indication of when a response may be expected. A full response must, in any event, be given within three months (Direction 6(1)).

(3) These time limits would, almost certainly, be regarded by a court as mandatory and would, accordingly, justify judicial review if breached (see, though, the tactical considerations in relation to judicial review at

para 8.7). The authority is required by Direction 9 to record whether the time limit has been complied with.

(4) The authority must notify in writing the result of its consideration to: (i) the complainant, (ii) (where different) the person on whose behalf the complaint was made 'unless the local authority consider that that person is not able to understand it or it would cause him unnecessary distress', and (iii) any other person who the authority considers has 'sufficient interest' in the case (Direction 7(1)). It is unclear who could fall within category (ii) above given that the complainant is, by Direction 2(1) expressed to mean a 'qualifying individual' under s 7B(2) of the Local Authority Social Services Act 1970 (see *above*), and only such persons have standing to invoke the complaints procedures at all. Furthermore, it is unclear as to why only that category of persons is exempt from notification in the event of incapacity to understand or distress. However, persons having a 'sufficient interest' is a potentially wide class and probably extends to anyone affected by or involved in the response. Although the Directions do not expressly so stipulate, the authority's response should advise the complainant what further options are open should he remain dissatisfied (see Appendix 3 for Policy Guidance, para 6.14).

(5) There is no express requirement in the Directions for the authority's notification to be reasoned, but this may be thought to be implicit in the obligation to notify 'the result of their consideration' in writing.

(6) Arrangements must be made so that where a complainant asks (within 28 days of notification) for the authority's response to be reviewed, a panel constituted by the authority meets within 28 days of the authority's receipt of the complainant's request (see Direction 7(2) and (3)). So far as the authority is concerned the time limits would probably be regarded by a court as mandatory and give rise, potentially, to judicial review if breached. It seems likely that an authority has a discretion to extend time for the complainant to seek review by the authority's panel in the interests of fairness.

(7) The authority must record its own notification and whether it (and, presumably, the complainant) has complied with the time limits in respect of the meeting of the panel (Direction 9).

Investigation of a complaint, at the registration stage, may need to be conducted by an investigator. The legal principles relevant to the type of enquiry to be conducted are similar to those in respect of assessment enquiries (see Chapter 3). A useful practice guide is contained as an Appendix to the Right to Complain and is reproduced in Appendix 3. Although the practice guide does not itself require the investigator's report or recommendations to the authority to be disclosed to the complainant, it is submitted that the complainant is entitled to disclosure of such material in order that he may comment upon it to the authority. In the absence of disclosure judicial review may lie since the complainant has not, in that event, been entitled to put his case properly or to make informed representations on matters that might be of concern to the investigator (see *R v Mental Health Review Tribunal, ex p Clatworthy* [1985] 3 All ER 699). This is particularly so given that the complainant is entitled to an oral hearing (see *below*) before the review panel and the investigator's report may be highly relevant to the representations that a complainant wishes to make before the panel.

The Complaints Procedure Directions 1990 are reproduced at Appendix 2.

7.6   The review stage

The review stage is the final stage of the stipulated complaints procedure and arises where a complaint has not been satisfactorily resolved at either the informal or registration stages. It involves formal consideration of the complaint by a panel of the authority.

Direction 2(1) of the 1990 Directions defines 'panel' as meaning a panel of three persons at least one of whom must be an independent person. Direction 2(3) defines 'independent person' as 'a person who is neither a member nor an officer of that authority, nor where the local authority have delegated any of its social services functions to any organisation, a person who is a member of or employed by that organisation, nor the spouse of any such person'. It is the 'independent person' who should chair the panel (see Policy Guidance, Annex A, para 4). (Helpful guidance as to how local authorities have selected an independent person is contained at paras 4.22 *et seq* of the Right to Complain.)

As indicated above, the review panel should meet within 28 days of the user's request for review. The panel has the task of reconsidering the authority's notification. It seems clear that the panel is engaged in a reconsideration of the notification decision rather than in a process akin to judicial review since Direction 7(3) of the 1990 Directions requires the panel to consider the matter together with any oral or written submissions as the complainant or the local authority wish it to consider.

It is also plain from the wording of Direction 7(3) that the complainant is, in contrast to the usual procedure at the registration stage, entitled to an oral hearing. This is reinforced by Annex A of the Policy Guidance at para 5 which advises that complainants should be notified in writing at least ten days beforehand of the time and venue of the meeting and that they should be invited to attend.

The conduct of the hearing is informal. Complainants should be told of their right to be accompanied by a representative. The Policy Guidance (Annex A, para 5) indicates that a representative should not be a professional barrister or solicitor but it is submitted that professional representation may be justified if difficult points of law might be involved and that a panel would err in law if it held that, in view of the Policy Guidance, it had no discretion to allow professional representatives to attend (see, eg, *R v Home Secretary, ex p Tarrant* [1985] QB 251). Care should be taken to ensure that particular disabilities or language difficulties are catered for so as to ensure fairness.

The regulation of procedure before the panel is, in principle, at the tribunal's discretion. However, a complainant or his representative should be permitted to make oral representations prior to the local authority. Other persons may, subject to the consent of the panel, attend part of the proceedings to make further submissions but will normally only be allowed to attend the hearing whilst making such submissions (Policy Guidance, Annex A at para 5). Clearly, the making of oral submissions does not affect a complainant's right to make representations in writing additionally or alternatively (see Direction 7(3)).

The panel is required to decide on its recommendations and record them in writing within 24 hours of the end of the meeting (Direction 8(1)). However, if it decides to take into consideration a matter on which it has not heard submissions it should alert the complainant and accord to him an opportunity of being heard (see *R v Mental Health Review Tribunal, ex p Clatworthy* [1985] 3 All ER 699). It must send written copies of its recommendations to:

(a) the local authority,

(b) the complainant,

(c) (if appropriate), the person on whose behalf the representations were made; and

(d) any other person who the local authority considers has sufficient interest in the case (Direction 8(2)).

The reasons for the panel's recommendations must be recorded in writing (Direction 8(3)) and, presumably (though the Directions are unclear) communicated to the same persons to whom the recommendations are sent (as indicated in para 7 of Annex A to the Policy Guidance). If a panel member disagrees with the majority recommendation, the letter should record that member's view and the reason for it (Policy Guidance, Annex A).

An authority is not bound to accept the recommendations of the panel. It has 28 days in which to decide whether to accept such recommendations and what action to take in the light of those recommendations (Direction 8(4)). As with the panel it should alert a complainant to any matter which it proposes to consider upon which it has not, through the panel, received submissions (see *R v Mental Health Review Tribunal, ex p Clatworthy* [1985] 3 All ER 699). The authority must, within that period, notify in writing the persons to whom the recommendations were sent of its decision/action and of their reasons.

Clearly, any errors of law or unfairness of procedure during the review stage will render the decision/action of the authority susceptible to judicial review. However, subject to the issue of whether judicial review may be sought as an alternative to invoking the complaints procedure at all, or as an alternative to following such procedure through to the review stage (see Chapter 8), if the complaints regime is utilised and taken to the final stage it is unlikely that an error of law or breach of natural justice at earlier stages of the procedure may be sought to be reviewed if the final review stage has been conducted lawfully and fairly (see *Calvin v Carr* [1980] AC 574; *Lloyd v McMahon* [1987] 2 WLR 821).

By virtue of Direction 9 of the 1990 Directions the local authority must record each representation received before the panel, together with the outcome both before the panel and before the authority. It must also record whether the time limits within which the panel and the local authority are, respectively, required to act at the review stage have been complied with. As with other time periods it is likely that failure to comply would be regarded as mandatory provisions although the practicalities of seeking judicial review in respect of non-compliance are dubious (see Chapter 8).

The relevant extracts from the Complaints Procedure Directions 1990, the Policy Guidance and the Right to Complain are reproduced at Appendices 2 and 3.

JUDICIAL REVIEW

8.1 Nature and scope of the remedy

Judicial review is a supervisory remedy whereby the High Court exercises control over the means by which public bodies perform their statutory duties and powers. The relevant procedure is contained in Order 53 of the Rules of the Supreme Court, and in s 31 of the Supreme Court Act 1981 (for an outline of the procedure see *below* at paras 8.8 *et seq*).

In the context of community care the scope of judicial review will extend, principally, to a local authority's procedures and decisions in respect of:

(a) entitlement to assessment (see Chapter 2);
(b) assessment (see Chapters 3, 5 and 6);
(c) service provision (see Chapters 4, 5 and 6);
(d) complaints by a qualifying individual (see Chapter 7).

Additionally, judicial review may lie if the Secretary of State has unlawfully exercised (or failed to exercise) his default powers (see Chapter 9) or, exceptionally, against unlawful directions or policy guidance issued by the Secretary of State (see Chapter 1).

Judicial review is a particular kind of remedy. It is concerned with legality rather than merits. As Lord Hailsham LC stated in *Chief Constable of North Wales Police v Evans* ([1982] 1 WLR 1155 at 1160):

> It is important to remember in every case that the purpose . . . is to ensure that the individual is given fair treatment by the authority to which he has been subjected and that it is no part of that purpose to substitute the opinion of the judiciary or of individual judges for that of the authority constituted by law to decide the matters in question.

It is also important to bear in mind that judicial review is discretionary. This means that even if a service user or other applicant establishes a *prima facie* case the High Court may still refuse relief. In community care cases the court may well refuse relief if it considers that an alternative remedy should have been utilised. Given the possibility, for example, of invoking the complaints regime or the Secretary of State's default powers where a local authority has reached an unfair assessment or service provision decision, an applicant and his legal advisers should carefully consider whether judicial review is a sensible immediate option to challenge such decision. This issue is considered at para 8.7 *below* and in Appendix 5.

The outline that follows is intended to clarify the grounds for judicial review and the remedies available, together with a summary of the main procedural provisions. Appendix 5 contains an exemplary case study.

8.2   Grounds for obtaining judicial review

In *Council of Civil Service Unions v Minister for the Civil Service* ([1985] AC 374) (the *CCSU* case) Lord Diplock (at 410) observed that:

> . . . one can conveniently classify under three heads the grounds upon which administrative action is subject to control by judicial review. The first ground I would call 'illegality', the second 'irrationality' and the third 'procedural impropriety'. That is not to say that further development on a case by case basis may not in course of time add further grounds.

The distinction between illegality and irrationality is nowhere better developed than in the judgment of Lord Greene MR in *Associated Provincial Picture Houses Ltd v Wednesbury Corporation* ([1948] 1 KB 223).

As to illegality he stated (at 233–234) that:

> The court is entitled to investigate the action of the local authority with a view to seeing whether they have taken into account matters which they ought not to take into account, or conversely, have refused to take into account matters which they ought to take into account.

He went on to observe (at 234), in respect of irrationality:

> Once that question is answered in favour of the local authority, it may be still possible to say that, although the local authority have kept within the four corners of the matters which they ought to consider, they have nevertheless come to a conclusion so unreasonable that no reasonable authority could ever have come to it. In such a case, again, I think the court can interfere.

Procedural impropriety is, essentially, non-observance of the rules of natural justice. This demands, in the context of the community care legislation, that a user is given a fair hearing. What constitutes a fair hearing will shift according to various factors that have already been considered (see Chapters 5 and 7) including, most notably, the subject matter of the assessment or complaint (see *Russell v Duke of Norfolk* [1949] 1 All ER 109 at 118, *per* Tucker LJ). The fairness of a hearing may also embrace the doctrine of legitimate expectation (see paras 5.3 and 7.2). Additionally, the time within which a decision is communicated and whether such decision is adequately reasoned are facets of natural justice albeit that they follow the hearing itself (see Chapter 6).

8.3   Available remedies

The following final forms of relief are, under Order 53, r 1, obtainable on judicial review:

(a)   the prerogative orders of *certiorari*, prohibition or mandamus;

(b)   a declaration or injunction.

It is also possible for damages to be awarded, but only as a private as opposed to a public law remedy. This is demonstrated by the requirement under Order 53, r 7(1) that the court determining the application for judicial review must be satisfied that damages could have been awarded at the time of making the application if, instead of seeking judicial review, the proceedings had been commenced by action.

In its modern form *certiorari* lies to quash a decision for invalidity. Prohibition prevents a local authority (or other respondent) from acting unlawfully. Mandamus requires performance of a specific duty in public law. These remedies can only be obtained by way of final order, (see s 29 of the Supreme Court Act 1981). The interim equivalent of prohibition and mandamus is the injunction (see para 8.4 *below*) which can also be obtained, though in practice it is rarely sought, as a final order. A declaration, as in private law, lies to declare the law though it, too, lies solely as a final form of relief (see *IRC v Rossminster* [1980] AC 952, *per* Lord Wilberforce at 1000).

The normal remedies in respect of allegedly unlawful assessment/service provision or complaints decisions will be *certiorari* to quash the decision and mandamus to require redetermination of the user's application according to law.

If the authority's decision ought, on its own reasoning, to compel service provision or the acceptance of the user's complaint then it may be possible to argue that the court should, on judicial review, order the authority (in addition to quashing the decision) to remit the matter to the authority with a direction to reconsider it and reach a decision in accordance with the findings of the court (see Order 53, r 9(4)). However, a direction of this kind is rare and would appear to be less apposite to assessment decisions which, by their nature, are less specific in point of determination.

It would generally be premature for a user to seek prohibition to prevent an authority from arriving at a particular decision but such circumstances might arise where, for example, a manifestly unlawful procedure was being followed to the user's detriment.

Failure on the part of a local authority to give a decision, or reasons therefor, or to review a decision would be reviewable by means of an order of mandamus (see *R v Home Secretary, ex p Phansopkar* [1976] QB 606).

Declaratory relief, rather than a prerogative order, is likely to be relevant if application is made against the Secretary of State in respect of directions or policy guidance because *certiorari* applies to 'judicial' rather than legislative action (see Wade, *Administrative Law*, (OUP) 1988 6th edn, p 876). Where the Secretary of State has unlawfully refused to exercise his default powers, the correct remedy would be *certiorari* to quash such decision and mandamus to compel exercise of the power. An unlawful exercise of default powers might involve a local authority in seeking, on judicial review, *certiorari* and prohibition to prevent the continued exercise of the power. In both these cases, however, declaratory relief would also be appropriate.

8.4   Interim relief on judicial review

In order to obtain interlocutory injunctive relief in judicial review an applicant must show that he has a real prospect of success at the hearing and that the balance of convenience favours the making of such order. In the case of a mandatory injunction it is necessary to show a strong *prima facie* case of breach of duty (see *R v Kensington and Chelsea Royal London Borough Council, ex p Hammell* [1989] QB 518). Undertakings as to damages will usually be required although the court has jurisdiction not to require such undertaking (see *R v London Borough of Lambeth and Caballito Properties Ltd, ex p Sibyll Walter*, unreported, 2 February 1989).

In a community care (as in a homelessness) case the need for interim relief will usually lie in respect of maintenance (or continued maintenance) of service provision. It is submitted that, in an appropriately strong case, the court may be prepared to grant interim injunctive relief to compel service provision. This is especially likely (so as to preserve the status quo) where community care services have been provided and are then withdrawn. It is, inde the prospect of obtaining such interim relief that justifies the use of judicial rather than exhausting other alternative remedies (see para 8.7 *below*).'v

Special considerations govern interim relief against the Secretary of St Interim injunctive relief is not obtainable (see *Factortame v Secretary of State Transport* [1990] 2 AC 85). However, the court does have jurisdiction to orde a stay of proceedings (equivalent to a prohibitory injunction) under Order 53, r 3(10)(a) against the Crown (see *R v Secretary of State for Education, ex p Avon County Council* [1991] 1 QB 558). This could certainly be used, in favour of a local authority, to prevent continued exercise of default powers pending a judicial review application although it would not avail a service user to compel exercise of such powers on an interim basis.

8.5 Discretion to refuse relief

Because of the discretionary nature of judicial review it cannot be assumed that victory is assured to an otherwise meritorious applicant. In community care cases the most likely reasons for relief being refused in the court's discretion are: (i) delay; and (ii) the existence of an alternative remedy. These are considered *below*.

However, relief may also be refused for a variety of discretionary reasons. The most usual bases are: because of an applicant's conduct (*Fulbrook v Berkshire Magistrates' Courts Committee* (1970) 69 LGR 75), or waiver (*R v Williams, ex p Phillips* [1914] 1 KB 608); or because the court does not discern the need for any order, as where a remedy is considered to be futile (*R v Secretary of State for Social Services, ex p Association of Metropolitan Authorities* [1986] 1 WLR 1), or unnecessary (*R v Monopolies and Mergers Commission, ex p Argyll Group Plc* [1986] 1 WLR 763). These factors are by no means exhaustive (see, eg, *R v Secretary of State for Social Services, ex p Cotton* (1985), *The Times*, 14 December: relief refused because it would be 'administratively inconvenient').

8.6 Delay

Order 53, r 4(1) provides that an application for leave to move for judicial review 'shall be made promptly and in any event within three months from the date when grounds for the application first arose unless the Court considers that there is good reason for extending the period within which the application shall be made'.

This provision must be read with s 31(6) of the Supreme Court Act 1981, which stipulates that where the court considers that there has been undue delay in applying for judicial review it may refuse to grant leave to make the application or any relief sought 'if it considers that the granting of the relief sought would be likely to cause substantial hardship to, or substantially prejudice the rights of, any person or would be detrimental to good administration'.

At the leave stage an applicant must show an arguable case. Generally the application is made *ex parte* (see para 8.9 *below*). In *R v Stratford-on-Avon District Council, ex p Jackson* ([1985] 1 WLR 1319) the court held as follows:

(1) An application for leave may be made within three months, yet still not be made 'promptly' so as to be out of time.

(2) In deciding whether to extend time the court should not be influenced by criteria applicable to private law cases; the fact that an applicant has had difficulty in obtaining legal aid will provide a good reason to extend time.

(3) Any application for leave made outside the three-month outer time limit will constitute 'undue delay' within the meaning of s 31(6) of the Supreme Court Act 1981 so that the court's discretion to extend time will need to be invoked.

In *R v Dairy Produce Quotas Tribunal, ex p Caswell* ([1990] 2 WLR 1320), the House of Lords approved the above reasoning and upheld the following general test:

(1) At the leave stage the judge must refuse leave if the application is not made promptly or within three months, unless the applicant establishes good reason to extend time.

(2) Even if the judge would otherwise have extended time he may refuse leave if he considers that there is substantial hardship/prejudice or detriment to good administration under s 31(6) of the Supreme Court Act 1981.

(3) In practice leave will usually grant leave, if good reason is shown, leaving the issue of prejudice, etc to be decided at the full hearing.

In community care cases, the most usual reason for delay will be the length of time in processing an applicant's legal aid application. As the decision in *Jackson* shows (see *above*), this will usually provide a sufficient reason for extending time although delay on the part of an applicant's solicitor in obtaining legal aid cannot be relied upon (see, eg, *R v Tavistock General Commissioners, ex p Worth* [1985] STC 564).

Care should be taken in pursuing other remedies such as an authority's complaints machinery or default powers of the Secretary of State.

Whilst the court is likely to consider that prior resort to other (not necessarily alternative) remedies affords a good reason for extending time for applying for leave to move, it would be sensible for those advising applicants either to extract a concession from the local authority that it will not take a time point if subsequent application for judicial review proves to be necessary or, alternatively, to lodge an application for leave to move but invite the court to adjourn it while the other remedies are pursued (see: Ord 53, r 3(8) by way of analogy).

8.7   Alternative remedies

The existence of an alternative remedy is not, of itself, a basis for refusing judicial review. Such remedy may not be designed to achieve the same objective as review. For example, a right of appeal often relates to merits rather than to legality.

Where, however, a free standing alternative remedy does exist the court's views will be determined by whether such remedy is legally more convenient. Convenience is dictated not only for the parties but also in the public interest (see *R v Huntingdon District Council, ex p Cowan* [1984] 1 WLR 501).

A useful case for those advising service user applicants is *Re Waldron* ([1986] QB 824). There (at 852) Glidewell LJ held that choice of remedy ought to depend upon whether an alternative statutory remedy:

(a) would resolve the question fully;
(b) would be quicker;
(c) demanded special knowledge.

The major problem facing applicants in community care cases will be whether to invoke a local authority's statutory complaints procedure or to seek judicial review.

It seems clear that the courts would regard the complaints regime as constituting an alternative remedy to judicial review since the statutory machinery is expressly designed to assist complaints 'in relation to the discharge of, or any failure to discharge' any of an authority's social services functions in respect of particular applicants (see s 7A of the Local Authority Social Services Act 1970). The same cannot be said of an authority's power to review a previous assessment/service provision decision, or the Secretary of State's default powers (as to the latter see Chapter 9).

Whilst the complaints regime might well resolve a complaint fully and require a degree of specialised knowledge, it is submitted that the determining factor in whether an applicant should proceed through the complaints machinery or seek judicial review is the availability of interim service provision.

Certainly, an authority has power to provide services in emergency cases (see National Health Service and Community Care Act 1990, s 47(5), and para 1.3). There is, however, no ostensible power to provide services where a decision has been taken not to do so under the s 47 of the 1990 Act. Such cases are, *ex hypothesi*, not emergency cases and to provide interim services would contradict the authority's own decision.

In those circumstances, assuming the applicant to have a strong *prima facie* case, judicial review (together with an expedited hearing) may be quicker in providing community care services given the availability of interim injunctive relief under Order 53 (see para 8.4 *above*) and should be applied for additionally or alternatively to participating in the complaints regime unless the authority agrees to provide services pending the resolution of the applicant's complaint.

8.8   Outline of the judicial review procedure

There are three stages to a judicial review application. These are:

(a)   the application for leave to move;
(b)   the interlocutory stage;
(c)   the final hearing.

(For a detailed exposition of the judicial review procedure, see: Gordon, *Crown Office Proceedings* (Sweet & Maxwell) 1990.)

8.9   Application for leave to move for judicial review

The application for leave is usually made *ex parte*. It is designed to satisfy the court that the applicant has an arguable case. As Lord Diplock succinctly expressed it in *IRC v National Federation of Self-Employed and Small Businesses Ltd* ([1982] AC 617 at 644):

If, on a quick perusal of the material then available, the court thinks that it discloses what might on further consideration turn out to be an arguable case in favour of granting to the applicant the relief claimed, it ought, in the exercise of a judicial discretion, to give him leave to apply for that relief. The discretion that the court is exercising at this stage is not the same as that which it is called upon to exercise when all the evidence is in and the matter has been fully argued at the hearing of the application.

An applicant is required to seek leave to move for judicial review, under Order 53, r 3(2), by filing in the Crown Office of the High Court:

— a notice in Form 86A (see Appendix 5);
— a supporting affidavit verifying the facts relied on (see Appendix 5).

Such application may be made *ex parte* 'on the papers'. This merely entails waiting for the decision of a High Court judge on the papers filed in the Crown Office. If the judge refuses leave the applicant may:

(a) renew the application by lodging Form 86B (see Appendix 5) in the Crown Office within ten days of notice of refusal of leave under Order 53, r 3(5): an oral *ex parte* hearing before a High Court judge will then be fixed by the Crown Office;

(b) further renew (if unsuccessful) to the Court of Appeal within seven days of refusal of leave at the oral hearing, under Order 59, r 14(3): different documents are required to bring the matter before the Court of Appeal for oral hearing.

It is possible to seek an oral rather than a paper hearing initially. If so, this must be requested expressly in Form 86A (see Ord 53, r 3(3)). Such oral hearing may be *ex parte* although there is a growing practice of serving the respondent so that he may assist the court. In the latter event an 'opposed *ex parte*' hearing takes place with the respondent making brief submissions before the single judge as to why leave should not be granted or, as appropriate, interim relief should not be granted. If an applicant is unsuccessful at the oral hearing stage his only further recourse is to renew to the Court of Appeal within seven days (see *above*).

The decision whether to seek an oral or paper hearing often involves tactical considerations. However, where interim relief is being sought an oral hearing should always be requested and the papers served on the respondent prior to seeking leave. This was emphasised in *R v Kensington and Chelsea Royal London Borough Council, ex p Hammell* ([1989] QB 518) where (at 539), Parker LJ observed as follows:

... where an application for interim relief is intended to be made, the applicant would be well advised to give notice to the other party that such an application is being made in order that the other party may, if he so wishes, attend and assist the court by filling in any gaps in the information that may be available and thereby enable the matter to be dealt with properly at a first hearing and dispense with the necessity of having a second hearing. I can, therefore, say no more than that notice that an *ex parte* application for interim relief is going to be made would be an advisable step in all cases.

Applicants in community care cases will frequently require an expedited hearing since, otherwise, there is often a year or more to wait between the grant of leave to move and the full hearing. If expedition is obtained the court should be asked to abridge time for service of the respondent's evidence from the usual 56 days to a lesser period so as to enable expedition to take place as soon as possible (see *Practice Note (Judicial Review: Affidavit in Reply)* [1989] 1 WLR 358).

8.10 The interlocutory stage

The papers (Form 86A/affidavit/notice of motion) must be served on the respondent and other persons 'directly affected' by the decision complained of within 14 days following the grant of leave. They must also be lodged in the Crown Office within that period together with an affidavit of service (see, generally, Ord 53, r 5).

Most forms of interlocutory relief are available in judicial review, including amendment of the Form 86A (see Ord 20, rr 7 and 8, and Ord 53, r 6(2)), and extension of time under Order 3, r 5. Application should be made on notice of motion to the court having jurisdiction to determine the substantive application. The motion should be supported by affidavit. Those interlocutory applications relating only to the movement of a case within the Crown Office List should be made to the Master of the Crown Office on summons supported by affidavit.

The most important applications from an applicant's point of view are:

(a) discovery and inspection under Order 24;
(b) leave to cross-examine the deponent of any affidavit under Order 38, r 2(3).

There is no automatic discovery in judicial review, and the case law indicates that discovery is more difficult to obtain under Order 53 than in a private law action (see *R v Secretary of State for the Home Office, ex p Harrison* [1988] 3 All ER

86). However, in an appropriate case discovery will be ordered. In the community care context it will frequently be important to know the basis upon which an assessment/service provision or complaint decision was made.

From a respondent's point of view the most important interlocutory applications are:

(1) Applications to set aside the grant of leave under Order 32, r 6, (such applications should be made only rarely where there has been material non-disclosure or where the applicant has no arguable case).

(2) Extension of time for filing affidavit evidence under Order 3, r 5, (such application should be made before the expiry of time for compliance).

Prior to the full hearing the applicant should prepare a paginated bundle of documents for the use of the court. It will also be important for the applicant's counsel to prepare a skeleton argument for the court three days before the hearing in accordance with the requirements of the 'active case letter' from the Crown Office (see Appendix 5).

If the case is compromised an agreed order may be handed in to the Crown Office signed by the parties. Because of the public law nature of the proceedings reasons must be given for any compromise (see *Practice Direction (Crown Office List: Uncontested Proceedings)* [1982] 1 WLR 979; see Appendix 5 for a precedent).

8.11   Final hearing

The full hearing consists of oral argument by both sides. Except where cross-examination is allowed (which is highly exceptional), the hearing will take the form of legal argument upon the Form 86A and affidavits.

Costs normally follow the event subject to the usual limitations imposed by the grant of a legal aid certificate. There is a right of appeal, without leave, to the Court of Appeal within 28 days of the sealing of the order.

Chapter 9

Default Powers of the Secretary
of State

9.1 Nature of the powers

Section 50 of the National Health Service and Community Care Act 1990 inserts a new s 7D into the Local Authority Social Services Act 1970. By s 7D(1) of the 1970 Act if the Secretary of State is satisfied that any local authority has failed, without reasonable excuse, to comply with any of its duties which are social services functions (other than a duty under the Children Act 1989), he may make an order declaring that authority to be in default with respect to the duty in question.

Any declaration made under s 7D(1) may be supplemented by directions requiring the local authority to comply with its duty within such specified period as the Secretary of State considers is necessary (see s 7D(2)). Any direction not complied with is enforceable, at the suit of the Secretary of State, by mandamus (s 7D(3)).

The default power under s 7D is characteristic of many similar powers in social services legislation generally. In the context of challenging assessment or service provision decisions or, indeed, the manner in which an authority has responded to a complaint it is clear that a local authority is exercising a social services function. Thus, invoking the default powers of the Secretary of State may be a potential alternative remedy to judicial review (but see *below*).

In this chapter the following questions are considered:

(1) Which of the local authority's social services functions are susceptible to exercise of the default powers?
(2) What constitutes a 'reasonable excuse' so as to prevent the Secretary of State from exercising his default powers?
(3) Are default powers an alternative remedy to judicial review?

(4) Does the existence of a default power preclude the bringing of a private law action?

(5) What remedy does an applicant have if the Secretary of State refuses to exercise his default powers?

9.2 Functions subject to default powers

Section 7D(1) of the Local Authority Social Services Act 1970 applies to 'duties' which are social services functions. Axiomatically, there is a fundamental distinction in administrative law between a duty and a power. Thus, in circumstances in which a local authority has a discretion as opposed to a duty to exercise a particular social services function the default powers of the Secretary of State cannot be exercised under the 1970 Act.

In relation to assessment, service provision and complaint adjudication many of the social services functions required to be performed by local authorities are mandatory and are, therefore, subject to exercise of the Secretary of State's default powers.

The duties of a local authority under s 47 of the 1990 Act are:

(a) to carry out an assessment (s 47(1)(a));

(b) to decide, in the light of the assessment, whether an individual's needs call for the provision by the authority of particular community care services (s 47(1)(b)).

Clearly, also, an authority has a duty, at least in public law, to provide services which it decides that an individual's needs call for it to provide.

In respect of complaints, a local authority has a duty to establish a complaints procedure and to administer it (see s 7B of the Local Authority Social Services Act 1970).

However, a local authority has a measure of discretion as to its conclusions on assessment (see Chapter 3), as to service provision decisions (see Chapter 4), and as to complaints decisions (see Chapter 7). Whilst it is true that discretionary powers must not be abused so as to thwart the policy of an Act of Parliament, (see *Padfield v Minister of Agriculture, Fisheries and Food* [1968] AC 997), it is submitted that the default power machinery is not intended to regulate the manner in which a local authority exercises its discretion even where it is contended that discretionary powers have been abused. Default powers are intended to be exercised in respect of statutory duties that have not been complied with as opposed to the duty that the common law imposes not to abuse statutory discretion.

This view is supported by the expression 'without reasonable excuse' (see *below*) set out in s 7D(1). The notion of the Secretary of State examining the legality of the manner in which a local authority has exercised its discretion, and the authority seeking to provide a reasonable excuse for such exercise, is contrary to the purpose of the default power regime which is 'an administrative device of last resort which is rarely used and which has as its object the internal efficiency of the executive machinery of the State' (see Wade, *Administrative Law*, (OUP) 1988, 6th edn, p 749).

9.3   Reasonable excuse

A local authority may seek to excuse non-performance of a social services statutory duty. If, in the Secretary of State's view, the authority's explanation of non-compliance is reasonable then he may not exercise the default power.

It is apparent that what constitutes a reasonable excuse is, generally, for the Secretary of State to determine in his discretion (see s 7D(1) which begins: 'if the Secretary of State is satisfied . . .').

It is, largely, a question of fact. Certainly, ignorance of or mistake concerning the statutory requirement cannot provide a reasonable excuse for non-compliance (see, eg, *R v Reid (Philip)* [1973] 1 WLR 1283).

However, lack of resources may well constitute a reasonable excuse for non-provision of services that the authority has determined it must provide even if it is no defence to judicial review proceedings seeking declaratory relief that such duty is owed (see Chapter 4).

9.4   Alternative remedy?

It is apparent from the above discussion that default power cannot constitute an alternative remedy to judicial review.

The only likely circumstances, in the present context, in which default powers might be apposite would be where a local authority has simply refused to assess or to create a complaints regime or to provide services in respect of which it had the resources and a duty to provide or where it had plainly disregarded a direction of the Secretary of State.

It does not follow from this, however, that the default power machinery, even where applicable, truly constitutes an alternative remedy to judicial review. As already observed, default powers are not really a species of legal remedy at all, and certainly not equally convenient so as to preclude judicial review (see *R v Leicester Guardians* [1899] 2 QB 632 at 639, *per* Darling J). They are '. . . suitable for dealing with a general breakdown of some public service caused by a local authority's default, but . . . quite unsuitable as a remedy for defaults in individual cases . . .' (Wade, *Administrative Law*, (OUP) 1988 6th edn, p 749).

9.5 Default powers and actions for damages

It is sometimes said that the courts will not intervene if Parliament has provided another remedy even if this prevents individuals from bringing actions for breach of statutory duty.

Two cases—*Wyatt v Hillingdon London Borough Council* ((1978) 76 LGR 727) and *Southwark London Borough Council v Williams* ([1971] Ch 734)—are often cited. In both instances private law rights contended for by individuals were held by the courts to be enforceable solely by means of specific default procedures vested in the Secretary of State.

However, a better explanation of the *Wyatt* and *Southwark* cases is that the nature of the duty sought to be enforced in place of a particular default power made it unsuitable for enforcement in private law at all. If an authority's failure to provide services is actionable in private law (for which see Chapter 10) then the existence of an independent default procedure ought, in principle, to be irrelevant (see, eg, *Meade v Haringey LBC* [1979] 1 WLR 637). The more difficult question, examined in Chapter 10, is whether an authority's failure to provide services can afford an individual right to damages.

9.6 Failure to exercise default powers

If the Secretary of State irrationally fails to exercise his default powers he is himself potentially amenable to judicial review (see, eg *R v Secretary of State for the Environment, ex p Ward* [1984] 1 WLR 834). Probably, standing for judicial review would not be restricted to those persons directly owed duties under the 1990 Act, (see *ex p Ward, above*).

Chapter 10

Action for Damages

10.1 The problems

None of the remedies discussed in Chapters 7 to 9 are designed to result in an award of damages for a service user unlawfully deprived of community care services although, presumably, a local authority could, at its discretion, make a payment of compensation following adjudication of a complaint made to it.

In order to obtain compensation through the courts a service user would have to establish a cause of action in private law against the authority. In theory this might arise out of:

(a) an enforceable claim by reason of a direct breach of statutory duty ('breach of statutory duty'); and/or

(b) a claim arising out of a decision of the authority to provide particular services to an individual and then not providing such services ('executive action'): such claim derives from the premise that an action for breach of statutory duty arises once a service provision decision in the applicant's favour has been made.

The difficulty under either of the above heads is that an action for damages for non-provision of services can only be based on a breach of statutory duty. However, in this area of the law few actionable rights are created. Nothing in the National Health Service and Community Care Act 1990 expressly removes this difficulty or opens the way for additional damages actions merely by creating an individual assessment regime, although it is possible that the duties to assess and reach a service provision decision themselves create actionable claims for damages in private law if breached (see *below*).

The important question is whether the courts will construe s 47 of the 1990

Act so as to let in damages claims where a local authority makes a service provision decision in the applicant's favour but then fails or refuses to provide the service.

10.2 Breach of statutory duty

The 1990 Act in no way alters the pre-existing duty imposed, or power conferred, on a local authority to provide 'community care services'. Thus, for example, the duty to provide after-care services under s 117 of the Mental Health Act 1983 subsists independently of the new assessment regime that the 1990 Act has introduced.

Of the various statutes that set out the range of 'community care services' (see s 46(3) of the 1990 Act), it has been said that s 117 of the Mental Health Act 1983 is an exception to statutory provisions that 'read more like general duties to provide certain services for people in the area' than duties owed to particular individuals (see Brenda Hoggett, *Mental Health Law*, (Sweet & Maxwell) 1990, 3rd edn, p 307).

If this analysis is right it follows that, *prima facie*, an individual formerly unable to bring a private law claim for breach of statutory duty in respect of non-provision of what are now 'community care services' is not entitled to bring such action merely because the 1990 Act creates a needs-assessed service provision decision-making process (unless, perhaps, an authority fails to assess or make any decision at all; see *below*).

10.3 Executive action

Different considerations may apply, however, once a service provision decision is made in the applicant's favour.

Section 47(1)(b) of the 1990 Act creates a duty to make a decision as to whether an individual's needs call for service provision by the authority. The ostensible duty is simply one of arriving at a decision. However, following an authority's decision that it is called upon to provide particular community care services it is arguable that there is a further implied duty in private law (there is almost certainly a public law duty) to provide such services and that failure to do so gives rise to an actionable claim against the authority for damages for breach of statutory duty.

Certainly, the Laming letter (see Appendix 3 at para 13) assumes such liability for it indicates that

> . . . once the authority has indicated that a service should be provided to meet an individual's needs and the authority is under a legal obligation to provide it or arrange for its provision then the service must be provided. . . .

Provided that s 47(1) of the 1990 Act does create such implied obligation (the point is not free from doubt) Lord Bridge's analysis in *Cocks v Thanet District Council* ([1983] 2 AC 286) (see para 4.7) applies. The starting point for a damages claim will be the stage at which the authority reaches its service provision decision.

If a service provision decision is taken that results in the withdrawal of services it is difficult to spell out any corresponding statutory duty that would give rise to an action for damages. The rationale of executive action depends upon the authority making a decision and failing to give effect to it. If, however, the decision is subsequently replaced by a later decision, the first decision lapses and any 'rights' that a service user has in respect of an unlawful later decision lie in public law.

10.4   Interrelationship with other remedies

An application for damages may be joined to judicial review proceedings where there is a private as well as a public law claim (see para 8.3). This will undoubtedly be the case where an authority has failed to implement a favourable service provision since such failure renders the authority liable to mandamus as well as to a possible damages claim for breach of statutory duty.

Although the Secretary of State's default powers may properly be exercised in respect of an authority's failure to provide services where it has made a favourable service provision decision there is no reason in principle why, if a damages claim lies, it should not be proceeded with instead of or in addition to seeking the exercise of such powers (see para 9.5).

10.5   Other actions for breach of statutory duty

It is possible that an authority's failure to carry out an assessment at all or to make a service provision decision may give rise to a statutory duty, breach of which affords an individual the right to seek damages for breach of statutory duty. It is also possible that an authority's failure to set up a complaints machinery creates similar rights. Certainly, a failure by a local authority to implement its own complaint adjudication may give rise to private law rights in the same way as failure to provide services following a favourable service provision may do (see *above*).

PART 4

Financial Aspects of Assessment

CHAPTER 11

FINANCIAL ASPECTS OF COMMUNITY CARE

11.1   Scheme of the 1990 Act

The scheme of the National Health Service and Community Care Act 1990 is that services are to be provided in the most cost effective manner. Paragraph 5 of the DoE Circular (10/92) states:

> The Government's policy remains that care should be provided to people as far as possible in their existing housing where this is their preference and it is practicable and cost effective to do so.

Furthermore, the providers of services may be able to recover all or part of the cost of that care from the resident.

In this chapter the following questions are examined:

(1) How does an authority charge for its services?
(2) How much can the authority charge?
(3) How does an authority assess the means of a claimant?
(4) What role do benefits play?

11.2   Charging for services: accommodation

Under s 22 (1) of the National Assistance Act 1948, as modified by s 44 of the 1990 Act, a local authority is obliged to recover a payment from the person for whom accommodation is provided. (The exception to this is where accommodation is provided for a child under 16 who is accompanied by an adult. The accompanying adult is liable for the cost of the accommodation for both of them.) The obligation to charge also applies where accommodation is provided under s 29 in a hostel managed by the local authority. Generally, the accommodation charge is to be set at the so-called 'standard rate'. This standard rate is calculated by the local authority and must reflect the full cost of providing particular accommodation to a particular individual. Thus, it is submitted that it is unlawful to set a standard rate that represents anything other than the exact cost: no more and no less.

The general policy is that a resident is to be charged according to his means. In no case, however, are a resident's resources after payment of the accommodation charge to be reduced below the personal requirements allowance, which at the time of writing is £10.85 per week.

Nevertheless, if the accommodation provided is in premises actually managed by the authority there is a discretion, exerciseable for up to eight weeks, to limit the resident's liability to pay for the accommodation. In these circumstances, the authority has power, irrespective of the resident's finances, to charge him such sum as it is reasonable to expect him to pay.

In all cases where accommodation is provided in premises maintained by voluntary organisations, the person becomes liable to reimburse the local authority for the full amount that the authority has paid the voluntary organisation for his accommodation. As with those cases where the authority itself has provided the accommodation, the authority must assess the means of the applicant to determine how much of the total cost he can afford.

11.3   Means assessment

The processes and procedures a local authority must embark upon in order to assess the means a claimant are now set out in the National Assistance (Assessment of Resources) Regulations 1992 (SI No 2977) ('the Assessment Regulations').

Under the regulations there are two systems for the calculation of means. There are the 'new rules' and the 'old rules'. The old rules apply under the transitional provisions which apply to cases of persons being temporarily absent from accommodation between 1 and 11 April 1993 and in some cases beyond. The application of the old rules is therefore very limited and is not considered in this book.

A person's income is calculated weekly and in two parts. First, by determining the weekly net income. Second, by adding to that figure a notional sum for the income from any capital.

11.4   Income: the self-employed

The self-employed's gross earnings are his gross receipts of employment. Curiously, where the claimant is employed in providing boarding accommodation for which a charge is made, any payment by way of such a charge is not counted as earnings. (Special provision is made for the treatment of royalties or other periodic payments in respect of copyright.)

A self-employed person's earnings are his net profit. The weekly income for a self-employed person is his average weekly profit from that occupation over a period of 52 weeks. Sometimes, a person will have been self-employed for less than 52 weeks. In such cases, the authority may use a figure of less than 52 weeks, so as to select a figure which gives true reflection of the average weekly earnings.

However, not all a self-employed earner's earnings are to be included in the calculation of the average weekly income. Authorities are required to disregard earnings paid after self-employment has ceased.

11.5   Income: the employed

The employed applicant's earnings consist of any remuneration or profit derived from his employment. This includes:

— any bonus or commission;
— any payment in lieu of remuneration (except periodic sums for redundancy);
— payments in lieu of notice;
— holiday pay (except that which is payable more than four weeks after termination of employment);
— any retainer;
— expenses payments not wholly, exclusively and necessarily incurred in work. (Examples include travel between the home and the place of work, or the cost of a child minder while away at work during the day, etc.);
— compensation for unfair dismissal;
— arrears of pay, protective awards and other sums ordered to be paid under the Employment Protection Consolidation Act 1978;
— statutory sick pay.

Earnings do not, however, include any payment in kind, occupational pension, or expenses which arise wholly, exclusively and necessarily in connection with employment.

However, an authority is to disregard from earnings wages paid or due to be paid in respect of terminated or interrupted employment.

After a figure for gross earnings has been arrived at, it becomes necessary to make deductions for income tax, national insurance contributions and an allowance of one half of the weekly contributions towards an occupational or personal pension scheme.

11.6 Income other than earnings and benefits

All a resident's income is to be considered in the assessment. For example, the payment of an annuity is treated as income. This means that, save as excluded in Sched 3, Part I to the Assessment Regulations, all the applicants benefits are considered.

Additionally, if there is any capital liable to be repaid to the applicant by instalments and those instalments are outstanding at the first date on which the applicant becomes liable to pay a charge for his accommodation (or at the end of the period an authority has charged merely the 'reasonable sum'), then if the sum of those instalments and the residents capital exceed the £5,000 currently prescribed by reg 41(1) of the Income Support Regulations 1987 (SI No 1967), those instalments are treated as income.

Where it comes to the attention of an authority that a person has deprived himself of income in order to reduce his liability to pay the accommodation charge, the authority must include in his income calculation the income he has deprived himself of (cf the position with deprived capital).

The applicant has the notional income under regs 42(2) and (4) of the Income Support Regulations. Notional income consists of income which would become available if the claimant applied for it. This income is treated as being received by the claimant from the date on which it could be expected to be acquired were an application made. The exceptions to the notional income rule are the following sources of income:

(a) a discretionary trust;
(b) a trust fund of monies from a personal injury payment;
(c) unemployment benefit for those not required to work;
(d) certain increases in child benefit.

Notional income does not include income payments from the Macfarlane Trust, the Macfarlane (Special Payments) Trust, the Macfarlane (Special Payments)(No 2) Trust or the Independent Living Fund. It does include benefit payments to families in respect of a family member (who is the resident), where that payment is derived from the various Benefit Acts, a war disablement pension or war widow's pension. Any such items which are taken into account when the standard rate was set.

11.7   Calculation of the average weekly income

Where an employed earner receives income, it is to be apportioned over the period it was payable in respect of, in order to determine an average weekly income. There are complex provisions in reg 18 for selecting an artificial period where the income does not correspond to a particular period.

In general, the following produce the weekly income:

(1) Where the apportionment period does not exceed one week, it is assumed that that payment relates to one week and this produces the average weekly income.
(2) Where the payment relates to a month, the weekly average is found by multiplying that payment by 12 and dividing the product by 52.
(3) Where the period is a seasonal quarter, by dividing the amount by 13 weeks
(4) Where the period is one year, by dividing by 52.
(5) In any other case by multiplying the payment by seven and dividing the product by the number of days the payment was in respect of.

11.8   Capital

No applicant shall be assessed as unable to pay at the standard rate if his capital exceeds what is stipulated in reg 45 of the Income Support Regulations, currently £8,000. This is on the basis that a person with such capital should use those resources first, before relying upon public funds to pay for his accommodation.

However, not all capital is to be included in the assessment. Sched 4 to the regulations lists those items of capital that are to be disregarded. In other cases, income is to be treated as capital. These situations are as follows:

(a) any bounty save for the first £15 of the following earnings:
   (i) part-time fireman in a fire service maintained under the Fire Services Acts;
   (ii) auxilliary coastguard;
   (iii) person who mans lifeboats;

    (iv) territorial or reserve forces;
(b) tax refunds under Schedule D or E;
(c) holiday pay (except that payable four weeks after termination);
(d) income derived from capital is treated as capital from date it is due;
(e) advances or loans made by employers;
(f) any payment made by a local authority which represents arrears of payment under para 15 of Schedule 1 to the Children Act 1989;
(g) one-off charitable payments that are not from the Fund, the Macfarlane Trust, the Macfarlane (Special Payments) Trust, the Macfarlane (Special Payments)(No 2) Trust or the Independent Living Fund.

Capital within the UK is valued at its current market or surrender value, whichever is the higher, less a 10 per cent allowance for sale costs (if there are to be any). Such values must of course allow for any encumbrances on the asset.

National Savings Certificates are calculated to include their increase in value in most cases. If the certificate is in respect of an issue of certificates which by the last 1 July before the resident's accommodation was provided, the certificate is valued at its realisation price as if it had been bought on the very last day that issue of certificate was available for purchase. The effect of this is that if an applicant bought a certificate on 2 July 1991 and on 2 July 1993 he is given accommodation, the certificate was no longer available for purchase after 1 July 1993. The certificate is valued as if it had been bought on 30 June 1993 and sold on 1 July 1993. The crucial date is the date the issue ceased to be available. If the issue has not ceased to be available, the value is assumed to be the purchase price.

Capital outside the UK is valued in accordance with reg 50 of the Income Support Regulations.

11.9   Notional capital

Where a person deprives himself of capital so as to reduce his liability to pay the accommodation charge, that capital may be included in the calculation, except where:

(a) that capital is placed on trust for the applicant and is in respect of a personal injury; or
(b) capital is reduced under reg 26 of the Assessment Regulations (see *below*).

A resident may be treated as possessing any payment of capital which would be so treated under reg 51(2)(3) of the Income Support Regulations read as if reference to Sched 10 was a reference to Sched 4.

Regulation 51 (3)(a)(ii) was rewritten to catch any other capital item taken into account in setting the standard rate.

In order to prevent reductions in a person's liability where that liablity is discharged by another authority via an arrangement between two authorities, the payment by one authority to the other is regarded as belonging to the applicant as capital.

Regulation 26 provides that if the addition of notional capital to the actual capital results in a liability to pay for accommodation at a higher rate than would have been the case without the notional capital, the notional capital shall be reduced by the differnce between the rate he would have paid and the higher rate. On recalculation, this will produce a compromise rate between the two.

11.10   Joint capital

Joint capital is calculated in two ways depending upon whether the asset is an interest in land. In non-land cases, the asset is treated as if it was equally shared by the owners, regardless of the true position. The applicant's capital is the value of his share. In cases involving land, the applicant's capital is calculated as his actual share in the proceeds of a sale to a willing buyer (at the time of assessment), less 10 per cent for selling costs and less any encumbrance.

11.11   Income from capital

Regulation 53 of the Income Support Regulations and reg 28 of the Assessment Regulations provide for the calculation of income generated by capital at a tariff rate as follows:

> 53.—(1) Where the claimant's capital calculated in accordance with this Part exceeds £3,000 it shall be treated as equivalent to a weekly income of £1 for each complete £250 in excess of £3,000 but not exceeding £6,000.

> (2) Notwithstanding paragraph (1), where any part of the excess is not a complete £250 that part shall be treated as equivalent to a weekly income of £1.

(3) For the purposes of paragraph (1), capital includes any income treated as capital under regulations 24(2), 48 and 60 (charitable or voluntary payments, income treated as capital and liable relative payments treated as capital).

*   *   *

28. A resident's tariff income from capital shall be calculated in accordance with the method prescribed in regulation 53 of the Income Support Regulations (amended by regulation 13 of SI 1988/2022 and regulation 5(2) of SI 1990/671) (calculation of tariff income from capital), except that for the purposes of this regulation the references in regulation 53(3) of the Income Support Regulations to regulations 48 and 60 of the Income Support Regulations (income treated as capital and liable relative payments treated as capital) shall be construed as references to regulations 22 and 34 of these Regulations (income treated as capital and liable relative payments treated as capital) respectively.

11.12   Liable relatives

These are spouses or former spouses of a resident. Payments by them to the resident are to be treated as income. The manner in which they fall to be treated, however, depends upon the categorisation of the payment into: (i) periodical; or (ii) other than periodical.

11.12.1   Periodical

These are payments that are made or due to be made (and whether in advance or in arrears) to the resident at regular intervals pursuant to court order or maintenance agreement, or otherwise in an established pattern. This does not include payments before the resident was provided with accommodation.

Periodical payments are taken into account as follows. Where the intervals between payments are regular, the payment is taken into account over the length of one of those intervals. In other cases, the number of weeks is calculated by dividing the payment by the weekly amount. The weekly amount is calculated according to the period. If the period is less than one week, then the weekly amount is one. If the period is in months, the number of months are multiplied by 12 and divided by 52, to produce a weekly amount. In all other cases the weekly amount is arrived at by dividing the period with its number of weeks.

11.12.2   Other than periodical

Calculate the difference between the standard rate for the accommodation and the lower rate the resident would have paid but for the payment. Divide the payment by the difference. The result is the number of weeks over which the payment is to be taken into account.

Special provisions in reg 32 apply when a relative makes both a periodic payment and another payment concurrently and the weekly amount of the periodical payment calculated under reg 33 is less than the divisor.

Payments made to residents by liable relatives shall be treated as income unless the provisions of reg 34 apply. In such an event the payment will be treated as capital. This requires concurrent payments and the weekly amount of the periodic payment is equal to or exceeds the divisor.

11.13   Students

A student's main income will usually be his grant or a covenant from his parents/guardians. For assessment purposes, that income is not considered a charitable or voluntary payment and fails to be considered. Only that part of his grant/covenant that represents the standard maintenance grant is taken into account. That sum is then apportioned over the number of study weeks reflected in the grant or the period in respect of which it is payable if this is more or less than the period of study.

Student loans are considered in the ordinary way under reg 66A of the Income Support Regulations. Access payments that have been made are treated as charitable or voluntary payments. Access payments that have not yet been made are treated as capital.

11.14   Benefits: the effects

It has already been observed that most benefits, subject to exclusion, will be taken into account in determining on a resident's income and ability to pay the standard rate. There is, however, an effect of a decision that a person requires residential care that has not been mentioned hitherto. The consequence is that a person's income support will be reduced.

For those persons resident in care homes prior to 1 April 1993, there will be a 'preserved right' to the higher levels of income support. For those who do not have preserved rights, for example, those entering care homes after 1 April 1993, the level of income support will be reduced. Instead, there is to be a new 'residential allowance'. The rates for this allowance will be greater in London than the provinces.

It is also the case that other benefits will be affected. The right to housing benefit previously enjoyed by those in local authority accommodation will go. For specific details of the changes, see The Social Security Benefits (Amendments Consequential Upon the Introduction of Community Care) Regulations 1992 (SI No 3147).

APPENDICES

List of Abbreviations

The following documents are referred to in the Appendices by their shortened forms ('in brackets').

Care Management and Assessment: Managers' Guide ('Managers' Guide')
Caring for People, the government White Paper ('White Paper')
Circular CI (92) 34 ('The Laming letter')
Community Care in the Next Decade and Beyond: Policy Guidance ('Policy Guidance')
Joint Circular on Housing and Community Care, Circular 10/92 LAC (92) 12 ('Housing and Community Care Circular')
The Right to Complain: Practice Guidance on Complaints Procedures in Social Services Departments ('Right to Complain')

See para 1.7 in the main text for further details

These documents are Crown Copyright and these extracts are reproduced with the kind permission of the Controller of Her Majesty's Stationery Office.

Relevant Statutory Material

Contents

The material here reproduced is referred to in the main text

National Health Service and Community Care Act 1990

46.—(3) In this section—

'local authority' means the council of a county, a metropolitan district or a London borough or the Common Council of the City of London;

'community care services' means services which a local authority may provide or arrange to be provided under any of the following provisions—

    (a) Part III of the National Assistance Act 1948;

    (b) section 45 of the Health Services and Public Health Act 1968;

    (c) section 21 of and Schedule 8 to the National Health Service Act 1977; and

    (d) section 117 of the Mental Health Act 1983; and

'private carer' means a person who is not employed to provide the care in question by any body in the exercise of its functions under any enactment.

Assessment of needs for community care services

47.—(1) Subject to subsections (5) and (6) below, where it appears to a local authority that any person for whom they may provide or arrange for the provision of community care services may be in need of any such services, the authority—

    (a) shall carry out an assessment of his needs for those services; and

    (b) having regard to the results of that assessment, shall then decide whether his needs call for the provision by them of any such services.

(2) If at any time during the assessment of the needs of any person under subsection (1)(a) above it appears to a local authority that he is a disabled person, the authority—

    (a) shall proceed to make such a decision as to the services he requires as is mentioned in section 4 of the Disabled Persons (Services, Consultation and Representation) Act 1986 without his requesting them to do so under that section; and

(b) shall inform him that they will be doing so and of his rights under that Act.

(3) If at any time during the assessment of the needs of any person under subsection (1)(a) above, it appears to a local authority—

(a) that there may be a need for the provision to that person by such District Health Authority as may be determined in accordance with regulations of any services under the National Health Service Act 1977, or

(b) that there may be a need for the provision to him of any services which fall within the functions of a local housing authority (within the meaning of the Housing Act 1985) which is not the local authority carrying out the assessment,

the local authority shall notify that District Health Authority or local housing authority and invite them to assist, to such extent as is reasonable in the circumstances, in the making of the assessment; and, in making their decision as to the provision of the services needed for the person in question, the local authority shall take into account any services which are likely to be made available for him by that District Health Authority or local housing authority.

(4) The Secretary of State may give directions as to the manner in which an assessment under this section is to be carried out or the form it is to take but, subject to any such directions and to subsection (7) below, it shall be carried out in such manner and take such form as the local authority consider appropriate.

(5) Nothing in this section shall prevent a local authority from temporarily providing or arranging for the provision of community care services for any person without carrying out a prior assessment of his needs in accordance with the preceding provisions of this section if, in the opinion of the authority, the condition of that person is such that he requires those services as a matter of urgency.

(6) If, by virtue of subsection (5) above, community care services have been provided temporarily for any person as a matter of urgency, then, as soon as practicable thereafter, an assessment of his needs shall be made in accordance with the preceding provisions of this section.

(7) This section is without prejudice to section 3 of the Disabled Persons (Services, Consultation and Representation) Act 1986.

(8) In this section—
'disabled person' has the same meaning as in that Act; and
'local authority' and 'community care services' have the same meanings as in section 46 above.

* * *

Powers of the Secretary of State as respects social services functions of local authorities

50. After section 7 of the Local Authority Social Services Act 1970 (local authorities to exercise social services functions under guidance of the Secretary of State) there shall be inserted the following sections—

Directions by the Secretary of State as to exercise of social services functions

7A.—(1) Without prejudice to section 7 of this Act, every local authority shall exercise their social services functions in accordance with such directions as may be given to them under this section by the Secretary of State.

(2) Directions under this section—
  (a) shall be given in writing; and
  (b) may be given to a particular authority, or to authorities of a particular class, or to authorities generally.

Complaints procedure

7B.—(1) The Secretary of State may by order require local authorities to establish a procedure for considering any representations (including any complaints) which are made to them by a qualifying individual, or anyone acting on his behalf, in relation to the discharge of, or any failure to discharge, any of their social services functions in respect of that individual.

(2) In relation to a particular local authority, an individual is a qualifying individual for the purposes of subsection (1) above if—
  (a) the authority have a power or a duty to provide, or to secure the provision of, a service for him; and
  (b) his need or possible need for such a service has (by whatever means) come to the attention of the authority.

(3) A local authority shall comply with any directions given by the Secretary of State as to the procedure to be adopted in considering representations made as mentioned in subsection (1) above and as to the taking of such action as may be necessary in consequence of such representations.

(4) Local authorities shall give such publicity to any procedure established pursuant to this section as they consider appropriate.

Inquiries

7C.—(1) The Secretary of State may cause an inquiry to be held in any case where, whether on representations made to him or otherwise, he considers it advisable to do so in connection with the exercise by any local authority of any of their social services functions (except in so far as those functions relate to persons under the age of eighteen).

(2) Subsections (2) to (5) of section 250 of the Local Government Act 1972 (powers in relation to local inquiries) shall apply in relation to an inquiry under this section as they apply in relation to an inquiry under that section.

Default powers of Secretary of State as respects social services functions of local authorities

7D.—(1) If the Secretary of State is satisfied that any local authority have failed, without reasonable excuse, to comply with any of their duties which are social services functions (other than a duty imposed by or under the Children Act 1989), he may make an order declaring that authority to be in default with respect to the duty in question.

(2) An order under subsection (1) may contain such directions for the purpose of ensuring that the duty is complied with within such period as may be specified in the order as appear to the Secretary of State to be necessary.

(3) Any such direction shall, on the application of the Secretary of State, be enforceable by mandamus.

Grants to local authorities in respect of social services for the mentally ill

7E. The Secretary of State may, with the approval of the Treasury, make grants out of money provided by Parliament towards any expenses of local authorities incurred in connection with the exercise of their social services functions in relation to persons suffering from mental illness.

Local Authority Social Services Act 1970

Local authorities to exercise social services functions under guidance of Secretary of State

7.—(1) Local authorities shall, in the exercise of their social services functions, including the exercise of any discretion conferred by any relevant enactment, act under the general guidance of the Secretary of State.

Relevant Orders and Directions

Contents

The material here reproduced is referred to in the main text.

Local Authority Social Services (Complaints Procedure) Order 1990

1990 No 2244

The Secretary of State for Health, in exercise of the powers conferred by section 7B(1) of the Local Authority Social Services Act 1970, and of all other powers enabling him in that behalf, hereby makes the following Order:—

Citation and commencement

1. This Order may be cited as the Local Authority Social Services (Complaints Procedure) Order 1990 and shall come into force on 1st April 1991.

Complaints procedure

2. Every local authority shall establish a procedure for considering any representations (including any complaints) which are made to them by a qualifying individual, or anyone acting on his behalf, in relation to the discharge of, or any failure to discharge, any of their social services functions in respect of that individual.

Policy Guidance

Directions
Complaints Procedure Directions 1990
Arrangement of Directions

PART I—INTRODUCTORY

1 Interpretation
2 Citation and commencement

PART II—REPRESENTATIONS AND THEIR CONSIDERATION

3 Exclusions
4 Preliminaries
5 Local Authority action
6 Consideration by local authority
7 Notification to complainant and reference to panel
8 Recommendations

PART III—MONITORING OF OPERATION OF PROCEDURE

9 Monitoring of operation of procedure

PART IV—GENERAL

10 Exclusion from scope of procedures

The Secretary of State for Health, in the exercise of the powers conferred by section 7B(3) of the Local Authority Social Services Act 1970 (1970 c 42. Section 7B was inserted by section 50 of the National Health Service and Community Care Act 1990 (c 19)) and all other powers enabling him in that behalf, hereby gives the following directions to local authorities:

Part I—Introductory

CITATION AND COMMENCEMENT

1   These Directions may be cited as the Complaints Procedure Directions 1990 and shall come into force on 1st April 1991.

INTERPRETATION

2(1)   In these Directions, unless the content otherwise requires
'the Act' means the Local Authority Social Services Act 1970;
'complainant' means a person specified in section 7B(2) or anyone acting on his behalf, making any representation including a complaint to the local authority in relation to

the discharge of, or any failure to discharge, any of their social services functions in respect of that individual;

'independent person' has the meaning assigned by paragraph (3) and

'panel' means a panel of 3 persons at least one of whom must be an independent person as defined in paragraph (3);

'representations' means representations (including complaints) referred to in section 7B(1).

2(2)   In these Directions, unless the context requires otherwise—

(a)   any reference to a numbered section is to the section in the Act bearing that number,

(b)   any reference to a numbered direction is to the direction in these Directions bearing that number, and any reference to a numbered paragraph, is to the paragraph of that direction bearing that number.

2(3)   The expression 'independent person' in these Directions means a person who is neither a member nor an officer of that authority, nor, where the local authority have delegated any of its social services functions to any organisation, a person who is a member of or employed by that organisation, nor the spouse of any such person.

Part II—Representations and their Consideration

EXCLUSIONS

3   These Directions shall not apply to any representations, (including complaints) to which section 26(3) of the Children Act 1989 applies, made on or after the day upon which that section of the Act comes into force (a day has not yet been appointed for this section to come into force).

LOCAL AUTHORITY ACTION

4(1)   The local authority shall appoint one of their officers to assist the authority in the co-ordination of all aspects of their consideration of the representations.

4(2)   The local authority shall ensure that all members or officers involved in the handling of representations under section 7B(1) are familiar with the procedures set out in these Directions.

PRELIMINARIES

5(1)   Where a local authority receives representations from any complainant they shall attempt to resolve the matter informally.

5(2)   If the matter cannot be resolved to the satisfaction of the complainant, the local authority shall give or send to him an explanation of the procedure set out in these Directions and ask him to submit a written representation if he wishes to proceed.

5(3)   The local authority shall offer assistance and guidance to the complainant on the use of this procedure, or give advice on where he may obtain it.

CONSIDERATION BY LOCAL AUTHORITY

6(1)   The local authority shall consider the representations and formulate a response within 28 days of their receipt, or if this is not possible, explain to the complainant within that period why it is not possible and tell him when he can expect a response, which shall in any event be within 3 calendar months of receipt of the representations.

6(2)   The representations may be withdrawn at any stage by the complainant, in which case the procedure set out in these Directions (other than direction 9 and 11) shall no longer apply to that case.

NOTIFICATION OF COMPLAINANT AND REFERENCE TO PANEL

7(1)   The local authority shall notify in writing the result of their consideration to—
   (a) the complainant;
   (b) the person on whose behalf the representations were made, unless the local authority consider that that person is not able to understand it or it would cause him unnecessary distress;
   (c) any other person who the local authority considers has sufficient interest in the case.

7(2)   If the complainant informs the authority in writing within 28 days of the date on which the notification mentioned in paragraph (1) is sent to him that he is dissatisfied with that result and wishes the matter to be referred to a panel for review, the local authority shall appoint a panel (including any independent person) to consider the matter which the local authority shall refer to it.

7(3)   The panel shall meet within 28 days of the receipt of the complainant's request for review by the local authority to consider the matter together with any oral or written submissions as the complainant or the local authority wish the panel to consider.

RECOMMENDATIONS

8(1)   Where a panel meets under direction 7, it shall decide on its recommendations and record them in writing within 24 hours of the end of the meeting.

8(2)   The panel shall send written copies of their recommendations to—
   (a) the local authority,
   (b) the complainant,
   (c) if appropriate, the person on whose behalf the representations were made, and
   (d) any other person who the local authority considers has sufficient interest in the case.

8(3)   The panel shall record the reasons for their recommendations in writing.

8(4)   The local authority shall consider what action they ought to take, and notify in writing the persons specified in paragraph (1)(b), (c) and (d) of the local authority's decision and of their reasons for taking that decision and of any action which they have taken or propose to take within 28 days of the date of the panel's recommendation.

Part III—Monitoring

MONITORING OF OPERATION OF PROCEDURE

9   The local authority shall keep a record of each representation received, the outcome of each representation, and whether there was compliance with the time limits specified in directions 6(1), 7(3), and 8(1) and 8(4).

Part IV—General

EXCLUSION FROM SCOPE OF PROCEDURES

10   These Directions shall apply only to representations in respect of matters arising on or after the date when an order made under section 50 of the National Health Service and Community Care Act 1990 comes into force (1990 c 19).

Signed by authority of the Secretary of State for Health.

Minister of State for Health

National Assistance Act 1948 (Choice of Accommodation) Directions 1992

The Secretary of State in exercise of the powers conferred by section 7A of the Local Authority Social Services Act 1970 and of all other powers enabling her in that behalf hereby makes the following Directions:—

Citation, commencement and extent

1(1) These Directions may be cited as the National Assistance Act 1948 (Choice of Accommodation) Directions 1992 and shall come into force on 1st April 1993.

(2) These Directions extend only to England.

Local authorities to provide preferred accommodation

2   Where a local authority have assessed a person under section 47 of the National Health Service and Community Care Act 1990 (assessment) and have decided that

acommodation should be provided pursuant to section 21 of the National Assistance Act 1948 (provision of residential accommodation), the local authority shall, subject to paragraph 3 of these Directions, make arrangements for accommodation pursuant to section 21 for that person at the place of his choice within the United Kingdom (in these Directions called 'preferred accommodation') if he has indicated that he wishes to be accommodated in preferred accommodation.

Conditions for provision of preferred accommodation

3   Subject to paragraph 4 of these Directions the local authority shall only be required to make or continue to make arrangements for a person to be accommodated in his preferred accommodation if—

(a) the preferred accommodation appears to the authority to be suitable in relation to his needs as assessed by them;

(b) the cost of making arrangements for him at his preferred accommodation would not require the authority to pay more than they would usually expect to pay having regard to his assessed needs;

(c) the preferred accommodation is available;

(d) the persons in charge of the preferred accommodation provide it subject to the authority's usual terms and conditions, having regard to the nature of the accommodation, for providing accommodation for such a person under Part III of the National Assistance Act 1948.

Preferred accommodation outside local authority's usual limit

4(1) Subject to sub-paragraphs (2) and (3), paragraph 3(b) of these Directions shall not apply to a local authority which make arrangements which cost more than the local authority would usually expect to pay in order to provide a person with their preferred accommodation if a third party's contribution to that person (which is treated as that person's resources as assessed under the National Assistance (Assessment of Resources) Regulations 1992 is such that he can reasonably be expected to pay for the duration of the arrangements an amount which is at least equal to the difference between—

(a) the cost which the local authority would usually expect to pay for accommodation having regard to the person's assessed need, and

(b) the full standard rate for that accommodation as specified in section 22(2) of the National Assistance Act 1948 (liability to pay full cost of local authority accommodation, the 'standard rate') or pursuant to section 26(2) to (4) of that Act (liability to pay full cost of other accommodation arranged by local authority).

(2) Sub-paragraph (1) shall not apply in respect of cases in which the third party's contributions are made by a person who is liable under section 42 of the National Assistance Act 1948 to maintain the person who wishes to be provided with preferred accommodation.

(3) Nothing in these Directions shall prevent a local authority from making or continuing to make arrangements for a person to be accommodated in his preferred accommodation where the cost of making such arrangements is more than the local authority would usually expect to pay having regard to the person's assessed needs.

23 December 1992   Signed by authority of the Secretary of State

Guidance
National Assistance Act 1948 (Choice of Accommodation) Directions 1992

Purpose

1   Under new community care arrangements social services authorities will increasingly be making placements in residential and nursing home care. This direction is intended to ensure where that happens that people are able to exercise a genuine choice over where they live.

2   It also gives people the right to enter more expensive accommodation than they would otherwise have been offered if there is a third party willing and able to pay the difference in cost.

3   This direction is intended to formalise the best practice which most authorities would in any case have adopted. It sets out the minimum that individuals should be able to expect. It is not, however, intended to mark the limits of the choice that authorities may be able to offer people. Even where not required to act in a certain way by this direction, authorities should exercise their discretion in a way that maximises choice as far as possible within available resources.

Summary

4   If after an assessment of need an authority decides to provide residential care for someone either permanently or temporarily, it will make a placement on their behalf in suitable accommodation.

5   If the individual concerned expresses a preference for particular accommodation ('preferred accommodation') within the UK the authority must arrange for care in that accommodation, provided
- the accommodation is suitable in relation to the individual's assessed needs
- to do so would not cost the authority more than it would usually expect to pay for accommodation for someone with the individual's assessed needs
- the accommodation is available
- the person in charge of the accommodation is willing to provide accommodation subject to the authority's usual terms and conditions for such accommodation

6   If a resident requests it, the authority must also arrange for care in accommodation more expensive than it would normally fund provided there is a third party willing and able to pay the difference between the cost the authority would usually expect to pay and the actual cost of the accommodation.

Preferred Accommodation

7   As with all aspects of service provision, there should be a general presumption in favour of people being able to exercise choice over the service they receive. The limitations on authorities' legal obligation to provide preferred accommodation set out in the direction are not intended to deny people reasonable freedom of choice, but simply to ensure that authorities are able to fulfil their obligations for the quality of service provided and for value for money. The terms of the direction are explained more fully below. Where for any reason an authority decides not to arrange a place for someone in their preferred accommodation it must have a clear and reasonable justification for that decision which relates to the criteria of the direction.

SUITABILITY OF ACCOMMODATION

7.1   Suitability will depend on the authority's assessment of individual need. Each case must be considered on its merits.

7.2   Consequently accommodation will not necessarily be suitable simply because it satisfies registration standards. On the other hand accommodation will not necessarily be unsuitable simply because it fails to conform with the authority's preferred model of provision, or meet the letter of a standard service specification.

7.3   This direction does not affect Section 26(1D) of the National Assistance Act 1948 as inserted by the NHS and Community Care Act 1990 which prevents an authority making arrangements for residential care with anyone convicted of an offence under the Registered Homes Act 1984. Similarly, the direction does not require an authority to contract with any accommodation where for any other reason it is prevented by law from doing so.

COST

7.4   The test should be whether the cost of preferred accommodation is more than the authority would usually expect to pay for someone with the same assessed needs as the individual concerned. This is not necessarily the same as the cost that the authority would in fact have incurred had the particular individual not decided to exercise their right to choose, since that might be either higher or lower than the authority would usually pay. For example, the cost of a one particular placement at a given time might be determined by the fortuitous availability for whatever reason of a place below the cost that an authority would usually expect to meet, or else by the temporary unavailability of accommodation at the authority's usual price.

7.5   The costs being compared should be gross costs before income from charging. Given the different amounts that authorities will recover from individuals by way of charges it would not be possible to determine a usual net cost an authority would expect to pay.

7.6   Costs will vary around the country. There may be circumstances where an authority might judge the need to move to another part of the country to be an integral part of an individual's assessed needs (eg, in certain cases to be near a relative), and therefore one of the factors to be considered in determining what the authority would usually expect to pay.

7.7   Costs may also vary according to the type of care. For example, the cost an authority might usually expect to pay for respite care might be different from its usual cost for permanent care.

AVAILABILITY

7.8   A place in an individual's preferred accommodation may not always be available immediately. If the client wishes, authorities should where appropriate be willing to consider making temporary or intermediate arrangements until a place becomes available.

CONDITIONS

7.9   In order to ensure that they are able to exercise proper control over the use of their funds, authorities need to be able to impose certain technical conditions, for example in relation to payment regimes, review, access, monitoring, audit, record keeping, information sharing, insurance, sub-contracting etc.

7.10   The contract conditions required of preferred accommodation should be broadly the same as those it would impose on any other similar operation. Stricter conditions should never be used as a way of avoiding a placement. As with suitability, account should be taken of the nature and location of the accommodation. There may be reasons why it would be reasonable to adapt standard conditions and unreasonable not to. For example, authorities should take into account the fact that homes in other areas, or those which take residents from many areas, may have geared themselves to the normal requirements of other authorities.

7.11   In setting their usual terms and conditions authorities are reminded that Part II of the Local Government Act 1988 stipulates that they may not specify non-commercial considerations in contracts.

More expensive accommodation

8   The direction also places a duty on authorities to make placements in more expensive accommodation than they would usually expect to provided there is a third

party able and willing to pay the difference. A third party in this case might be a relative (but not a liable relative, see 11.13), a friend, or any other source.

9   This direction applies only where a resident explicitly chooses to enter accommodation other than that which the authority offers them, and where that preferred accommodation is more expensive than the authority would usually expect to pay.

10   This direction does not mean that authorities may set an arbitrary ceiling on the amount they are willing to contribute towards residential care and require third parties routinely to make up the difference. If challenged an authority would need to be able to demonstrate that its usual cost was sufficient to allow it to provide people with the level of service they could reasonably expect did the possibility of third party contributions not exist.

11   Similarly, the direction is not intended to allow authorities to require third party contributions in cases where the authority itself decides to offer someone a place in unusually expensive accommodation—for example, where there is at the time in question no suitable accommodation available at the authority's 'usual cost'.

RESPONSIBILITY FOR COSTS OF ACCOMMODATION

11.1   When making arrangements for residential care for an individual under the National Assistance Act 1948, an authority is responsible for the full cost of that accommodation. Therefore where an authority places someone in a more expensive accommodation it must contract to pay the accommodation's fees in full. The third party's contribution will be treated as part of the resident's income for charging purposes and the authority will be able to recover it in that way.

11.2   The prospective resident in these cases will therefore need to demonstrate that there is a third party able and willing to pay the difference between the authority's normal cost and the accommodation's actual fees.

11.3   In order to safeguard both residents and authorities from entering arrangements which are likely to fail, the third party must reasonably be expected to be able to continue to contribute for the duration of the arrangements. Authorities should assure themselves that there is every chance that the third party will continue to have the resources to make the required payments.

11.4   Authorities will be aware that under Section 26(3A) of the National Assistance Act 1948 (as inserted by the NHS and Community Care Act 1990), it is open to them to agree with both the resident and the person in charge of their accommodation that instead of paying a contribution to the authority, the resident may pay the same amount direct to the accommodation, with the authority paying the difference. In such a case the third party would also pay the accommodation direct on behalf of the resident. However, it should be noted that even where there is such an agreement for the resident to make direct payments, the authority continues to be liable to pay the full cost of the accommodation should either the resident or relative fail to pay the required amount.

11.5   Authorities should also note that because arrangements under section 26(3A) of the 1948 Act require the agreement of all parties, it would not be reasonable for them to refuse people their preferred accommodation on the grounds that they (or their preferred accommodation) would not enter such an arrangement.

THE AMOUNT OF THE THIRD PARTY CONTRIBUTION

11.6   The amount of the third party contribution should be the difference between the actual fee for the accommodation and the amount that otherwise the authority would usually have expected to pay for someone with the individual's assessed needs. In determining this amount the authority should apply the same consideration as above (7.4–7.8), except that in these cases it will need to state a precise figure in each case.

11.7   The amount of the third party contribution should be calculated on gross costs, ie the difference between the preferred accommodation's fees and the fees that an authority would usually expect to pay. The fact that residents might not have been able to meet the full cost of the accommodation that the authority would otherwise have arranged does not affect their ability to benefit from this part of the direction. When the third party's contribution has been taken into account, the cost net of charges to an authority of the more expensive accommodation should be the same as it would have been in accommodation at the authority's usual price.

PRICE INCREASES

11.8   Arrangements between the authority, resident and third party will need to be reviewed from time to time to take account of changes to the accommodation's fees and also changes to the amount the authority would usually expect to pay. These may not change at the same rate, and residents and third parties should be told that there cannot be a guarantee that any increases in the accommodation's fees will automatically be shared evenly between the authority and third party should the particular accommodation's fees rise more quickly than the costs the authority would usually expect to pay for similar people. An authority may find it useful to agree with the resident and third party that the third party's contribution will be reviewed on a regular basis.

RESPONSIBILITIES OF RESIDENTS AND THIRD PARTIES

11.9   Authorities should make clear to residents and third parties the basis on which arrangements are to be made when they seek to exercise their right to more expensive preferred accommodation. It should be clear from the outset to the resident, third party and person providing the accommodation

- that failure to keep up payments will normally result in the resident having to move to other accommodation
- that an increase in the resident's income will not necessarily lessen the need for a contribution, since the resident's own income will be subject to charging by the authority in the normal way
- that a rise in the accommodation's fees will not automatically be shared equally between authority and third party
- that if the accommodation fails to honour its contractual conditions, the authority must reserve the right to terminate the contract

11.10 Authorities may wish to consider making a binding legal agreement with the third party to this effect, though they should note there are restrictions on the ability of charitable contributors to enter into such contracts.

SUITABILITY AND CONDITIONS

11.11 The criteria of suitability, and willingness to provide on the basis of normal conditions should be applied in the same way as for other preferred accommodation (para 7.1 ff).

11.12 An exception to this is that it would be reasonable to expect providers entering this kind of arrangement to agree to do so on the basis that the authority has the right, subject to notice, to terminate the contract should the third party's payments cease or cease to be adequate.

LIABLE RELATIVES

11.13 Because they may already be obliged to contribute to the cost of accommodation, these arrangements do not apply to relatives liable to contribute to the cost of accommodation under section 42 of the National Assistance Act 1948. In other words, for the purposes of this direction such people cannot act as third parties for the care of the relative to whose care they are already obliged to contribute.

11.14 However, although the direction imposes no legal duty to do so, there is no reason why authorities should not enter in similar arrangements with liable relatives who have the resources both to meet their liability and make an additional third party payment. Indeed, there is no reason why authorities should not, at the request of the resident, arrange more expensive accommodation for someone who can from their own resources afford to pay the additional cost.

People already resident in residential care

12 People already placed by an authority in residential accommodation have the same rights under this direction as those who have yet to be placed. An individual who wishes to move to different or more expensive accommodation may seek to do so on the same basis as anyone about to enter residential care for the first time.

People who are unable to make their own choices

13   There will be cases in which prospective residents are unable to express a preference for themselves. It would be reasonable to expect authorities to act on the preferences expressed by their carers in the same way that they would on the resident's own wishes, unless exceptionally that would be against the best interests of the resident.

Effect on tendering, effect on block contracting

14   Many authorities will already be consulting on, or involved in formal tendering and contracting procedures. As this direction is intended simply to formalise best practice, there should be no conflict between it and arrangements authorities have already made.

15   However, authorities will need to review their arrangements to see if any further action is needed. In particular, where authorities have already published details of their contracting policies, they will need to inform prospective providers of any amendments to that policy required in the light of this direction.

16   For example, where authorities are conducting, or have completed, exercises designed to draw up closed lists of approved suppliers they will need to make it clear that as a result of this direction such a list cannot now be regarded as an exhaustive statement of those providers with whom the authority will contract. It would not be reasonable for an authority to use as a test of the suitability of accommodation its presence on or absence from a previously compiled list of approved suppliers. The direction does not, however, prevent an authority having a list of preferred providers with which it will contract where a potential resident expresses no preference for particular accommodation, nor from recommending such providers to prospective residents.

Information

17   For individuals to be able to exercise genuine choice they need information about the options open to them. They should be given fair and balanced information with which to make the best choice of accommodation. Authorities should explain to individuals their rights under this direction. Individuals should be told explicitly that they may allow the authority to make a placement decision on their behalf, that they may choose from a preferred list (if the authority operates such a system) or if they wish that they are free to choose any accommodation which is likely to meet their needs subject to the constraints set out in this direction. Authorities might consider including this in a leaflet for prospective residents and their carers.

Complaints

18   Complaints about the application of this direction and decisions taken in individual cases will fall within the scope of authorities' statutory complaints

procedures. As in all aspects of their activity, authorities should ensure that prospective residents are aware of the existence of the complaints procedure and of their rights under it.

EXTRACTS OF RELEVANT GUIDANCE

Contents

The guidance here reproduced is referred to in the main text.

White Paper

3.2.11   Each assessment should, of course, be handled on its merits, but simplicity should be the key. Contributions can be sought quickly and informally and it is not always necessary for all contributors to attend meetings. Assessments should be carried out timeously. The Government does not wish to see an elaborate and bureaucratic pattern of costly and time-consuming case conferences established, nor does it want to see a duplication of effort. For instance, where a patient has already been assessed for discharge from hospital, this should form the basis of the assessment decision.

ACTION FOLLOWING AN ASSESSMENT

3.2.12   The aim of assessment should be to arrive at a decision on whether services should be provided, and in what form. Assessment will therefore have to be made against a background of stated objectives and priorities determined by the local authority. Decisions on service provision will have to take account of what is available and affordable. Priority must be given to those whose needs are greatest. As part of its planning machinery, every local authority should monitor the outcomes of its assessment process, and the implications of these outcomes for future development of services.

Policy Guidance

Assessment

3.15   Although assessment is a service in its own right it can be distinguished from the services that are arranged as a consequence. The needs-led approach pre-supposes a progressive separation of assessment from service provision. Assessment does not take place in a vacuum: account needs to be taken of the local authority's criteria for determining when services should be provided, the types of service they have decided to make available and the overall range of services provided by other agencies, including health authorities.

3.16   The individual service user and normally, with his or her agreement, any carers should be involved throughout the assessment and care management process. They should feel that the process is aimed at meeting their wishes. Where a user is unable to participate actively it is even more important that he or she should be helped to understand what is involved and the intended outcome.

*   *   *

3.18   To enable users and carers to exercise genuine choice and participate in the assessment of their care needs and in the making of arrangements for meeting these needs, local authorities should publish readily accessible information about their care services. This should be compiled in consultation with health and housing authorities and other service providers. The information should cover residential care homes, nursing homes and other community care facilities available in all sectors. It should include the authority's criteria for determining when services should be provided and the assessment procedures, showing how and where to apply for an assessment and giving information about how to make representations and complaints.

*   *   *

3.20   Assessment arrangements should normally include an initial screening process to determine the appropriate form of assessment. Some people may need advice and assistance which do not call for a formal assessment, others may require only a limited or specialist assessment of specific needs, others may have urgent needs which require an immediate response. Procedures should be sufficiently comprehensive and flexible to cope with all levels and types of need presented by different client groups.

*   *   *

Care Plans

3.24   Once needs have been assessed, the services to be provided or arranged and the objectives of any intervention should be agreed in the form of a care plan. The objective of ensuring that service provision should, as far as possible, preserve or restore normal living implies the following order of preference in constructing care packages which may include health provision, both primary and specialist, housing provision and social services provision:

- support for the user in his or her own home including day and domiciliary care, respite care, the provision of disability equipment and adapatations to accommodation as necessary;
- a move to more suitable accommodation, which might be sheltered or very sheltered housing, together with the provision of social services support;
- a move to another private household i.e., to live with relatives or friends or as part of an adult fostering scheme;
- residential care;
- nursing home care;
- long-stay care in hospital.

3.25   The aim should be to secure the most cost-effective package of services that meets the user's care needs, taking account of the user's and carers' own preferences. Where supporting the user in a home of their own would provide a better quality of life, this is to be preferred to admission to residential or nursing home care. However, local authorities also have a responsibility to meet needs within the resources available and this will sometimes involve difficult decisions where it will be necessary to strike a balance between meeting the needs identified within available resources and meeting the care preferences of the individual. Where agreement between all the parties is not possible, the points of difference should be recorded. Failure to satisfy particular needs can result in even greater burdens on particular services, for example where a person becomes homeless as a result of leaving inappropriate accommodation which has been provided following discharge from hospital.

3.26   Decisions on service provision should include clear agreement about what is going to be done, by whom and by when, with clearly identified points of access to each of the relevant agencies for the service user, carers and for the care manager. No agency's resources should be committed without its prior agreement. However, where the agencies have agreed as a result of the assessment and care planning process to provide a service, they will be expected to deliver it. With the service user's permission, the assessment information should be passed on to those responsible for care delivery. This applies particularly to any risks that may be associated with the care of the user.

Carers

ROLE OF CARERS IN ASSESSMENT

3.27   Service users and carers should be informed of the result of the assessment and of any services to be provided. In the case of carers, due regard should be had to confidentiality, particularly where the carer is not a close relative. Where care needs are relatively straightforward the most appropriate way of conveying decisions can best be determined taking individual circumstances into account. A written statement will normally be needed if a continuing service is to be provided. Written statements should always be supplied on request.

3.28   Most support for vulnerable people is provided by families, friends and neighbours. The assessment will need to take account of the support that is available from such carers. They should feel that the overall provision of care is a shared responsibility between them and the statutory authorities and that the relationship between them is one of mutual support. The preferences of carers should be taken into account and their willingness to continue caring should not be assumed. Both service users and carers should therefore be consulted—separately, if either of them wishes— since their views may not coincide. The care plan should be the result of a constructive dialogue between service user, carer, social services staff and those of any other agency involved.

CARERS OWN NEEDS

3.29   Carers who feel they need community care services in their own right can ask for a separate assessment. This could arise if the care plan of the person for whom they care does not, in their view, adequately address the carer's own needs.

Rights of Disabled People

3.30   In accordance with Section 47(2) of the Act, if, at any time during their assessment, an individual is found to be a person to whom Section 29 of the National Assistance Act 1948 applies, the authority must so inform them, advise them of their rights and make a decision as to their need for services, as required by Section 4 of the Disabled Persons' (Services, Consultation and Representation) Act 1986. Once an individual's need for welfare services, specified in Section 2 of the Chronically Sick and Disabled Persons Act 1970, has been established, the authority must make necessary arrangements to meet it.

Charges for Services

3.31   Separate guidance will be issued in due course on the powers and duties of local authorities to charge for personal social services (including community care services). This will include the statutory charging arrangements under Section 22 of the 1948 Act for residential and nursing home care and discretionary schemes under Section 17 of the Health and Social Services and Social Security Adjudications Act 1983 for charges for welfare services. It is expected that local authorities will institute arrangements so that users of services of all types pay what they can reasonably afford towards their costs. But the provision of services, whether or not the local authority is under a statutory duty to make provision, should not be related to the ability of the user or their families to meet the costs, and delegated budgeting systems should take this into account. The assessment of financial means should, therefore, follow the assessment of need and decisions about service provision.

Collaboration with Other Agencies

3.32   Under the Act SSDs will have a legal duty to assess users' needs for community care services, that is welfare services provided under the enactments listed in Section 46(3) of the Act. However, the aim of assessment should be to ensure that all needs for care services are considered. Collaboration with health authorities and local housing authorities will therefore be of particular importance. Section 47(3) of the Act will require SSDs to bring apparent housing and health care needs to the attention of the appropriate authority and invite them to assist in the assessment. Arrangements for assessment and care management need to be addressed jointly by local agencies and roles and responsibilities agreed within those arrangements. As well as considering health and housing needs, staff from the local housing and health authorities may be able to offer expert advice on, and contribute to, the assessment of community care needs. Accommodation related needs, including the possible need for sheltered or very sheltered housing, will sometimes be an element in the assessment of community care need. The local authority is responsible for the involvement of all other agencies in deciding what should be done, by whom and by when, but other agencies will need to make available the staff needed for assessment. Information about the costs of community care services available from all agencies should, as far as possible, be made available to appropriate staff carrying out assessments, to assist them in arriving at cost-effective proposals.

3.33   All relevant agencies should be involved in the assessment process before commitments are made. It will be necessary to ensure that there are well-established links between SSDs, health authorities and local housing departments, particularly where urgent decisions may be needed. SSDs should recognise that the assessment process they originate may be used by other agencies to assist them in fulfilling their statutory responsibilities, for example by local housing authorities in assessing homelessness applications. Any requirements flowing from this should be taken into account in the assessment arrangements.

3.34   Where an individual's care needs appear to fall entirely outside the responsibility of the local authority it will usually be sufficient to refer the person to the appropriate agency and to notify that agency accordingly. A record should be made of such referrals. Care should be taken that individuals are not repeatedly referred from one agency to another.

3.35   Where a service user has complex needs, it may occasionally be necessary to call together staff from all the agencies concerned for a case conference; the individual and his or her carers should then be invited to attend. However, except in difficult cases, it should be possible to conduct consultations either informally in writing or by telephone (with a written record) to avoid delay and limit the demands on scarce professional skills. The number of people attending a conference should be kept small enough to permit a full exchange and appreciation of views.

Assessment of Nursing Care Needs

3.36   The statutory responsibilities of health authorities to meet health care needs are unchanged. This means that health authorities can continue to make contractual arrangements for nursing home placements, subject to local agreements. Detailed arrangements for care management and assessment will need to be developed locally to take account of the changes in the NHS which have resulted from 'Working for Patients', in particular the separation of the purchasing and providing functions.

3.37   The new arrangements create opportunities to assess the possibilities for supporting users with nursing care needs through community nursing services whether in their own homes, or in residential care homes, or in sheltered or very sheltered housing. Agreement will be needed between health and local authorities about the services each are to provide for such users and the criteria for admission to hospital, nursing home or other residential accommodations as part of the planning process. (See Chapter 2).

3.38   The Act requires SSDs to obtain health authority consent before placing users in nursing homes except in the case of arrangements made as a matter of urgency. This provision is aimed at assisting collaborative planning and at ensuring that nursing home care is chosen only when it is a better way of meeting the user's overall care needs than the use of the community nursing service or admission to hospital. It is expected that health authority approval will normally be obtained through participation in the assessment process.

3.39   Appropriate medical and nursing advice should always be sought when admission to residential or nursing home care is being considered. No changes are being made to procedures for admission to hospital. Short-term admission will have a positive role in providing for both acute care and rehabilitation.

Urgent Admissions to Residential or Nursing Home Care or to Hostels

3.40   Under the Act, services may be provided without assessment in cases where they are required urgently. Urgent admissions to nursing homes do not require the consent of the health authority. Authorities will need to negotiate arrangements for emergency care. Voluntary and private agencies providing such services on behalf of statutory authorities should be informed what resources they can commit and for how long without reference to the authority. Assessment must be carried out as soon as possible afterwards.

Hospital Admissions and Discharges

3.41   The decision to admit to, or to discharge from, hospital is taken primarily on medical grounds but it also has to take account of social and other factors. Wherever these factors come into play, there should be close consultation between health authorities and SSDs. It is most undesirable that anyone should be admitted to, or remain in, hospital when their care could be more appropriately provided elsewhere.

3.42   Local assessment arrangements for services required by a patient following discharge from hospital will need to be reviewed in the light of the new responsibilities local authorities will have. As explained in existing circulars on hospital discharge

(HC(89)5 and LAC(89)7) health authorities, in conjunction with local authorities, are responsible for designating staff to develop, implement and monitor individual discharge plans. To ensure the continuity of health and social care the local authority and NHS staff working in the community and GPs should be given adequate notice of discharge to enable them to assess and provide for any community care needs, especially where residential or nursing home care may be a possible choice. Local housing authorities may also need to be involved.

3.43   Health authorities should bear in mind that responsibility for assessing and meeting needs for community social services (including nursing home care where the user is expected to contribute to the cost) rests with the SSDs. Subject to any arrangements agreed between authorities, local authorities should not be expected to endorse decisions about an individual's care needs, or ways of meeting them, taken by health authorities in advance of a recognised community care assessment.

3.44   Subject always to consumer choice, patients should not leave hospital until the supply of at least essential community care services has been agreed with them, their carers and all the authorities concerned. Patients who have lost their homes should not be expected to leave hospital until suitable accommodation has been arranged. In such cases early liaison with the local housing authority is essential.

3.45   Further guidance on discharge from psychiatric hospitals is contained in Chapter 7 and in the forthcoming interdisciplinary guidelines for good practice in discharge and after-care procedures.

Family Health Services Authorities

3.46   Local Authorities will need to agree with FHSAs arrangements which ensure that the GP's contribution to the assessment of need can be brought to bear effectively. Both authorities should ensure that GPs are given sufficient information on assessment procedures to enable them to be involved effectively in the assessment process and to advise patients. In the preparation of the information FHSAs, on behalf of local authorities, should consult local professional committees. There should be no need for complex arrangements.

General Practitioners

3.47   It is expected that, as a matter of good practice, GPs will wish to make a full contribution to assessment. It is part of the GP's terms of service to give advice to enable patients to avail themselves of services provided by a local authority.

3.48   Where advice is needed by the local authority in the course of assessment, this should be obtained from the GP orally (eg by telephone) as far as possible. A record should be kept of the advice given. In addition to the information that only the patient's own GP can provide, local authorities may, on occasion, also require a clinical examination or an interpretation of the medical report provided by the GP. Local authorities should, therefore, be aware that GPs have a personal duty to and a relationship with their patients, and may not be best placed to act in addition as an assessor on the authority's behalf. In such circumstances local authorities may wish other practitioners to act in this capacity.

Role for Independent Agencies in Assessment

3.49   Where a specialist service—for example as at drug and alcohol centres—is provided by a voluntary body under arrangements with a SSD, it will be possible to include assessment of needs in relation to such services in contract arrangements. Voluntary organisations may, in addition, have a role in providing expert advice in assessments. Contracts may also provide for agencies to make decisions about service provision but, in such cases, contracts should include arrangements for the SSD to specify both the overall resources the agency may commit in this way and the maximum amount which may be spent on any one user. Formal overall responsibility for decisions on service provision will remain with the SSD, which will be responsible for assessing need for any additional services lying outside the specialist concern of the voluntary body.

Confidentiality of Health and Personal Social Services Information

3.50   The Data Protection Act 1984 and orders made under it, the Access to Personal Files Act 1987 and related regulations, and the Access to Health Records Act 1990 and the obligations to safeguard health and personal social services information, will affect the use authorities make of information they receive or hold, and the circumstances in which this can be disclosed. Proper assessment, the design of appropriate packages of care and the arrangement of services, will sometimes depend on agencies being able to share information. The need for this should be explained to the service user and his or her written consent first obtained. Detailed guidance is given in circulars LAC(87)10, LAC(88)16, LAC(88)17, HC(FP)(88)22 and LAC(89)2.

Review of Care Needs

3.51   Care needs, for which services are being provided, should be reviewed at regular intervals. This review, especially where it relates to complex needs, should wherever possible, be undertaken by someone, such as a care manager, not involves in direct service provision, to preserve the needs-led approach. The projected timing of the first review should be stated in the original care plan. However, reviews may take place earlier if it is clear that community care needs have changed. Reviews may also be needed of services already being provided before the introduction of the new arrangements.

3.52   The purpose of the review is to establish whether the objectives, set in the original care plan, are being, or have been met and to increase, revise or withdraw services accordingly. Reviews should also take account of any changes in needs or service delivery policies. The other purpose of reviews are to monitor the quality of services provided and, in particular, to note the views of service users and carers and any changes in their wishes or preferences. These views should be fed back into service planning, together with any identified shortfalls in provision.

3.53   The type of review will vary according to need but all those involved in the original care planning should be consulted. Large-scale review meetings should rarely be necessary. All relevant agencies, service users and carers should be notified of the results of the review, subject to the same constraints of confidentiality as the care plan.

*   *   *

Scope

6.5   The intention of the Act is to allow access to a statutory procedure to anyone who is likely to want to make representations, including complaints about the actions, decisions or apparent failings of a SSD; and to allow any other person to act on behalf of the individual concerned. The procedure excludes only those for whom the authority has no power or duty to provide a service. Complaints of a general nature which are not concerned with an individual case are also likely to fall outside the statutory definition, as are anonymous complaints. It will be open to authorities at their discretion to deal with a complaint not covered by Section 7B under the standard procedure.

*   *   *

Other Guidance

6.9   Authorities will be required within the statutory framework and in the light of the Department's guidance to devise or modify their own arrangements. This guidance is not exhaustive. In reviewing or setting up their procedures authorities may find it helpful to refer, for example, to the code of practice on complaints procedures issued by the Local Authority Associations and the Commission for Local Administration in 1978; and to the booklet 'Open to Complaints: guidelines for social services complaints procedures' published by the National Consumer Council (with the National Institute for Social Work) in 1988. Social Services Inspectorate practice guidance on the organisation and operation of procedures and on training will be published separately.

*   *   *

Complaints Procedure

ESSENTIAL REQUIREMENTS

6.14   The complaints procedures established by authorities should be uncomplicated, accessible to those who might wish to use them and understood by all members of staff. They should reflect the need for confidentiality at all stages. The essential requirements are contained in the directions at Appendix C. They require authorities to:

- designate an officer to assist in the co-ordination of all aspects of the consideration of complaints;
- ensure that the arrangements made clearly identify the key stages in the complaints procedure and the responsibility of staff at each of those stages;

- ensure that members and staff of the authority are familiar with the arrangements made, and that those arrangements clearly identify the key stages in the complaints procedure and the responsibility of staff at each of those stages;
- consider and respond to every registered complaint within 28 days of receipt of the complaint and, where this is not possible, give an explanation of the position to the complainant within the first 28 days and make a full response within 3 months;
- address their response to the person from whom the complaint was received, and also, where different, to the person on whose behalf the complaint was made and to any other persons who appear to have a sufficient interest or are otherwise involved or affected. The response should advise the complainant what further options are open should he or she remain dissatisfied;
- make arrangements so that where a complainant asks (within 28 days) for the authority's response to a registered complaint to be reviewed, a panel constituted by the authority meets within 28 days of the authority's receipt of the complainant's request;
- ensure that the panel's recommendation is recorded in writing within 24 hours of the completion of their deliberations; and is sent (formally) to the authority, to the complainant and to anyone acting on his behalf;
- decide on their response to the recommendation of a panel and make their decision known in writing to the person who requested the review, and where different, the person on whose behalf the request was made and any other persons as appear to have a sufficient interest or are otherwise involved or affected within 28 days of the date of the recommendation. The letter should explain the authority's decision and the reasons for it;
- keep a record of all complaints received and the outcome in each case; and identify separately those cases where the time limits imposed by the directions have been breached.

* * *

FORM OF COMPLAINT

6.17 There should be no requirement in the first instance for complaints to be written down. Where a complainant wishes to pursue a matter that cannot be resolved informally the complaint should, however, be made in writing, whether by the complainant or by someone (who might be a member of staff) on the complainant's behalf. It is at this point that a complaint is 'registered'.

* * *

Publicity

6.26 Service users, carers and their respresentatives will need to be properly informed about the authority's social services policy, the assessment process and criteria for service provision (see Chapter 3). The complaints procedure itself must be publicised, in accordance with Section 7B(4) of the 1970 Act. This requirement might be met by using:

- **Leaflets**
  These should explain the procedure in straightforward terms and should include a reference to the role of the Commissioner for Local Administration (the

Ombudsman) and to the separate leaflet 'Complaint about the Council?'. The leaflet should give the name, address and telephone number of the designated officer or of the person responsible for oversight of the procedure, and of organisations to whom those individuals might turn for advice. It should be made widely available. Where necessary, authorities will need to make available versions of their leaflet in ethnic minority languages and in braille.

- **Notices**
  These should be displayed in the authority's offices. They should also be supplied—with leaflets—to agencies offering independent advice.
- **Visual and oral presentations**
  Authorities may wish to discuss with voluntary organisations and other local groups how information about the complaints procedure should be made available to those with sensory handicaps, the housebound and those whose first language is not English or who do not speak English.

*   *   *

Support for Complainants

6.28   In setting up their complaints procedures, authorities will wish to consider how best to ensure provision of the support and encouragement service users and others will need if the procedure is to be effective. Direction 5(3) places a particular responsibility on authorities in this respect. Support may on occasions be provided from outside the authority. But making an immediate offer of help, and giving the complainant the opportunity to explain and discuss a concern when it first arises, the chances of resolving the matter there and then increase. A positive response of this kind will also allay any fears complainants might have about the consequences of voicing a complaint.

Assessment Decisions

6.29   The notification of the outcome of an assessment should include a reference to the complaints procedure. Where a complaint is subsequently received, the grounds for the decision made might first need to be reconsidered by the officer responsible for the assessment in the light of the matters raised in the complaint. The subsequent reply should say how the complaint may be pursued further. If the complainant remains dissatisfied, the complaint should then be registered and dealt with accordingly.

Special Cases

6.30   An inflexible application of the complaints procedure in all cases would clearly be inappropriate. There will be circumstances in which the earlier stages of the procedure should be bypassed; or an entirely different route taken. Where serious allegations are made senior staff will need to be involved at the outset. Where such allegations suggest that a criminal offence may have been committed the relevant local procedure, which may be contained in the authority's standing orders, should be followed. Where the allegation is serious and substantial the police must be notified immediately.

*   *   *

Elected Members

6.34 The complaints procedure should not affect in any way the right of an individual or organisation to approach a local councillor for advice or assistance. The procedure should, however, indicate clearly how complaints made to councillors which cannot be resolved on the spot should be handled.

Mental Health Act 1983

6.35 The Mental Health Act Commission has responsibility, under the Mental Health Act, for overseeing the detention and treatment of compulsorily detained patients; and a general responsibility for the care, treatment and after-care of all mentally disordered people. Mentally disordered people and their carers may complain directly to the Commission.

*　　*　　*

Annex A
Review Panels

1 The directions specify that the review panel appointed by the authority at the request of a person dissatisfied with a local authority's written response to his or her registered complaint should be made up of 3 people, at least one of whom should be an independent person.

2 Authorities may individually or jointly wish to draw up a list of independent persons suitable and willing to act as an independent member of a panel so that they can act quickly when the need arises. The people appointed should, where possible, have experience relevant to the subject matter of the complaint. The list should reflect the ethnic make up of the local population and should be prepared in consultation with voluntary groups, other agencies and perhaps independent professionals to ensure that independence is demonstrably built into the procedure. In some areas a standing panel appointed for a period (perhaps not exceeding 3 years) might be an effective arrangement. Otherwise a panel could be convened for each occasion.

3 Independent persons should be given a letter of appointment explaining the duties they will be required to carry out, describing the expenses and other payments to which they may be entitled and drawing attention to important issues such as confidentiality. Authorities will need to consider what training or other support they might wish to provide for independent persons and perhaps other panel members. (This might be dealt with by joint initiatives between authorities.)

4 The directions require the panel to meet within 28 days of the receipt of a request for a review. The designated officer might oversee arrangements for appointing the Chairman and other panel members and convening the meeting. The Chairman should be an independent person. Other members of the panel may be independent persons or councillors or other persons whom the authority consider suitable.

5   Complainants should be notified in writing at least 10 days beforehand of the time and venue of the meeting and be invited to attend. Complainants should also be informed of the name and status of the panel members, specifying which members are independent persons, which officers of the authority will be present, and of their right to make written submissions to the panel before the meeting and to make oral submissions at the meeting. Complainants should be told of their entitlement to be accompanied by another person who would be entitled to be present at the whole meeting and to speak on their behalf if they so wish. This person should not be a barrister or solicitor acting in a professional capacity. In arranging a meeting, the authority may need to consider what provision should be made for complainants whose first language may not be English, or those who may have mobility problems or special communication needs.

6   The meeting should be conducted as informally as possible. The chairman of the panel should open the meeting by explaining its purpose, proposed procedures, and with a reminder about confidentiality. The complainant (or a person accompanying him or her) should be given the opportunity to make an oral submission before the authority's representative does. Other people may attend the meeting to make oral submissions if requested to do so by the complainant, subject to the consent of the panel, but will normally only be allowed to be present for that part of the meeting.

7   The panel is required by direction to record its recommendation within 24 hours of the meeting and to notify in writing the complainant, the authority and where appropriate others with an interest. The letter of notification should explain simply and clearly the recommendations **and the reasons for them**. If a panel member disagrees with the majority recommendation the letter should also record that member's view, and the reason for it.

8   Under the terms of the system for payment of members' allowance which comes into force next year it will be possible for authorities to meet travelling and subsistence costs incurred by councillors in the course of their duties as members of review panels. Payment of attendance allowance will be governed by the definition of 'approved duties' which at present does not cover service on review panels. The Department is discussing with the Department of Environment a possible widening of the definition. Authorities will be notified of the result in due course.

9   Legislation will not specify the basis of payments to independent panel members who for this purpose could be regarded as consultants. Authorities are free to make arrangements in line with their usual practice.

10   Authorities are also free to decide whether to reimburse the travelling and other expenses of complainants, their representatives or anyone else attending review panels.

117

Managers' Guide

Section 2
Assessment arrangements

PUBLISHING INFORMATION

2.4 Authorities should be in a position to publish information about their **assessment practices** prior to April 1993.

2.5 This information should, as a matter of good practice, include:
- the range of needs for which the agency accepts responsibility
- the aims, priorities and objectives of the agency, partly derived from the national objectives set out in the policy guidance
- the types of services available from all sectors, setting out the range of needs for which they cater
- the criteria determining access to resources
- the referral, assessment and review procedures within and between agencies
- the entitlements of users and carers to information, participation and representation, including provision for equal opportunities
- the charging policies
- the standards by which the agency will monitor its performance, including response times to referrals
- complaints and feedback procedures.

*   *   *

ASSESSING NEED

2.20 Assessment staff will, wherever possible, cease to be linked to specific services. Instead, a **range of vocationally and professionally qualified staff** will be available to assess needs of differing levels of severity and complexity. Beyond them, there will be defined access to a range of specialist staff or to assessment staff in other agencies. The priority requirement for assessment staff will be an **indepth understanding of the needs** associated with particular user groups and a **knowledge of the range of services and community resources** available to meet those needs. In organisational terms, this is most likely to result in staff specialising in assessment/care management as distinct from service provision. However, alternatively, they may perform both functions but for different users or else rotate between the two roles, at specified intervals.

In order to undertake an assessment of need, staff have to know:
- the needs for which the agency accepts responsibility
- the needs for which other care agencies accept responsibility
- the needs of carers which qualify for assistance
- the agency's priorities in responding to needs
- the financial assessment criteria for determining users' contributions
- the agency's policy on risk to the user and to the community
- the legal requirements

*   *   *

Managers' Guide—Levels of assessment

Assessment	Needs	Services	Agency	Staff	Example of service outcome
1 Simple assessment	Simple, defined	Existing universal	Single	Reception or administrative	Bus pass Disabled car badge
2 Limited assessment	Limited, defined, low-risk	Existing, subject to clearly defined criteria	Single	Vocationally qualified	Low-level domiciliary support
3 Multiple assessment	Range of limited, defined, low-risk	Existing in a number of agencies	Multiple	Vocationally qualified or equivalent	Assistance with meals, chiropody and basic nursing
4 Specialist assessment					
(a) simple	Defined, specialist, low-risk	Existing, specialist	Single or multiple	Specialist ancillary	Simple disability equipment
(b) complex	Ill-defined, complex, high-risk	Existing and/or new specialist	Single or multiple	Specialist professional	Home adaptation
5 Complex assessment	Ill-defined, inter-related, complex, volatile, high-risk	Existing and/or new individual combinations of service	Single or multiple	Professionally qualified	Speech therapy
6 Comprehensive assessment	Ill-defined, multiple, inter-related, high-risk, severe	Existing and/or new individual combinations of service	Multiple	Professionally qualified and/or specialist professional	Family therapy Substitute care or intensive domiciliary support

2.24   In respect of simple needs, this may be done on a verbal basis but where an assessment results in the offer of a continuing service, this should normally be communicated in writing in the form of an individual care plan. The content of such plans are set out in the *Practitioners' Guide* (Stage 4 page 67). It should be noted that an assessment of users' financial means will have to be synchronised with the care planning process so that users are not asked to agree a care plan before knowing the financial cost to themselves.

The Laming letter

5   The principal duty relating to assessment is Section 47 of the 1990 Act, which states:

'**47**   (1) ... where it appears to a local authority that any person for whom they may provide or arrange for the provision of community care services may be in need of such services, the authority—

(a) shall carry out an assessment of his needs for those services

(b) having regard to the results of that assessment, shall then decide whether his needs call for the provision by them of any such services'.

Two important points should be noted about this:

- first, authorities do not have a duty to assess on request, but only where they think that the person may be in need of services they provide;
- second, the assessment of need and decisions about the services to be provided are separate stages in the process.

*   *   *

Level of Assessment

9   The type and level of assessment that is offered to an individual should relate to the level and complexity of need that is being presented, the aim being to keep the process as simple and efficient as possible. Most assessments are likely to be simple and straightforward. Staffing arrangements and documentation should reflect this. Comprehensive multi-agency assessments are both time consuming and expensive. They should normally be reserved for the minority of users with the most complex needs. A full scale assessment of all needs for community care services should be offered to individuals appearing to be disabled, as prescribed by Section 47(2) of the NHS and CC Act.

10   Authorities should, therefore, have:

(a) a procedure for screening or filtering referrals according to agreed criteria;

(b) published criteria for:

  i   identifying disabled persons under the terms of the legislation;

  ii   determining the appropriate type and level of assessment;

  iii   involving other agencies (see paragraph 19).

(c) staff with designated responsibility for operating these criteria.

*   *   *

Assessment and Service Provision

12   The assessment should focus on the difficulties for which individuals are seeking assistance, but it should take account of all the circumstances relevant to those individuals:

— their capacities and incapacities;
— their preferences and aspirations;
— their living situation;
— the support available from relatives and friends;
— any other sources of help.

This information then provides the context for subsequent decisions about what services (if any) will be provided.

13   An authority may take into account the resources available when deciding how to respond to an individual's assessment. However, once the authority has indicated that a service should be provided to meet an individual's needs and the authority is under a legal obligation to provide it or arrange for its provision then the service must be provided. It will not be possible for an authority to use budgeting difficulties as a basis for refusing to provide the service.

14   Authorities can be helped in this process by defining eligibility criteria ie a system of banding which assigns individuals to particular categories, depending on the extent of the difficulties they encounter in carrying out every day tasks and relating the level of response to the degree of such difficulties. Any 'banding' should not, however, be rigidly applied, as account needs to be taken of individual circumstances. Such eligibility criteria should be phrased in terms of the factors identified in the assessment process. (The Community Care Support Force has circulated examples of how a number of authorities have tackled this task). Authorities should ensure that all staff undertaking assessments understand and apply these criteria consistently.

15   As far as individual users are concerned, their care plans (of which they should receive a copy) should spell out the extent to which their needs qualify for assistance under the terms of the eligibility criteria. Care plans should also define the contribution to be made by each agency and professional towards the meeting of those individuals' needs.

*   *   *

31   The care plans of all users should be subject to regular review. For frail people in the community, frequent reviews and adjustments of their care plans are likely to be needed. Before any changes in services are made for existing users, they should be re-assessed. In those cases, where assessments have been undertaken, particularly under Section 2(1) of the CSDP Act 1970, authorities must satisfy themselves, before any reduction in service provision takes place that the user does not have a continuing need for it. So long as there is a continuing need, a service must be provided although, following review, it is possible that an assessed need might be met in a different way.

Right to Complain

Chapter 4
The Procedure Itself

(refers to the NHS and Community Care Act 1990 unless otherwise stated)

THE DETAILS OF THE PROCEDURE

4.1   There will be three stages to the procedure:
1—The Informal or Problem-Solving Stage;
2—The Formal or Registration Stage;
3—The Review Stage.

1—THE INFORMAL OR PROBLEM-SOLVING STAGE

4.2   Normal good practice should sort out, to the user's satisfaction, the queries and grumbles which are part of a social services department's daily workload. Stage 1 then alerts the relevant worker, supervisor or manager to the fact that there is a more fundamental problem, as perceived by the user or her or his representative. It gives users the right to decide whether or not to pursue the issue and ensures that it is taken seriously and not dismissed by busy staff.

4.3   The fact that this stage is not 'formal' does not mean that it is 'casual'. It may well be necessary to involve someone who is not connected with the immediate problem to help resolve it. This is where Clients' Relations Officers can be valuable (see also Chapter 6).

*   *   *

4.5   This is a means by which complaints can be sorted out without recourse to the more formal system. It should not be used as a device to prevent or dissuade users from making a formal complaint.

*   *   *

4.8   It is recommended that it is made clear to all concerned that the purpose is to solve problems at the earliest possible stage. To pursue every case to the final stage would undermine this concept.

2—THE FORMAL OR REGISTRATION STAGE

4.9   Stage 2 does not imply that problem-solving activities will be abandoned. It may involve investigation, adjudication and a decision or solution. If the complainant wishes, for any reason, to go straight to Stage 2 of the procedure s/he should be helped to do so.

4.10   To *'register'* a formal complaint, it will need to be put in writing either by the individual concerned or someone else on their behalf to the Designated Complaints Officer. Many people will need support and advice from someone they trust either from within or outside the department. Some people will need help in writing and sometimes in formulating a complaint. Those who give help in writing down the complaint must ensure that it fully reflects what the complainant wishes to say and ask the complainant to sign it.

* * *

4.13 When the report is received by the DCO, the manager or member responsible for the original decision should be given the opportunity to see it and take action on it. If, however, this cannot be done or agreement is not possible, senior management with the responsibility for the service concerned should take the decision about the department's response and the DCO will inform the complainant of the outcome and the department's decision. In relation to the children's complaints procedures, an independent person will be involved at Stage 2 (ie after the problem-solving stage), and may see appropriate papers and interview the people involved.

* * *

MEMBERSHIP OF THE PANEL

4.22 Some local authorities have used local voluntary organisations to help form the independent element of the panel eg Coventry SSD has approached Age Concern, MIND, and other local groups. Some authorities are considering the formation of consortia of suitable people drawn from a number of local authorities. In contrast, East Sussex have decided not to use former officers or members or people from other local authorities as members of the panel.

4.23 As stated in the policy guidance, it will be useful for the members of the panel to reflect the cultural diversity of the area and to have appropriate expertise or experience of the subject matter of the complaint. For example, if a particular disability or minority group is involved, the panel should be convened so that the complainant's concerns are responded to sensitively and appropriately.

4.24 Some SSDs have decided that all members of the review panel are to be 'independent' as defined in the policy guidance. Others have envisaged the panel with one elected member, one senior officer with management responsibility in the SSD and one independent member, who may be drawn from a range of voluntary organisations, depending on the type of complaint.

4.25 It is important to distinguish between the role of the 'independent person' in the complaints procedure from the task of those who help users and carers to pursue their complaint and are there specifically to support, advise and befriend and may well be from the voluntary sector.

4.26 The Children Act Representations Procedure (Children) Regulations 1991 allow the same independent person to be involved in the consideration of a complaint at both the formal and review stages of the procedure. However, it will be for local authorities to consider whether the panel will be able to take a fresh look at the complaint if the same independent person is involved at both stages.

* * *

Appendix A
Good Practice for Investigators

(Compiled with the help of the Office of the Commission for Local Administration (the local government ombudsman))

1   Check if there are any previous recorded formal complaints from this person;

2   Contact the complainant to:
   (a) clarify the complaint;
   (b) ask what is expected in terms of solution or outcome;
   (c) check whether s/he needs support of any kind
       whether s/he has poor sight or hearing, or a language difficulty;
       what s/he needs to understand the discussion properly (and try to ensure that this is provided);
   (d) explain the investigation procedure;

3   Read about the background and the relevant legal and administrative policies and procedures;

4   Assess whether the complaints procedure is the most appropriate way of handling this complaint. Consider alternative possible procedures, for example appeals to tribunals, legal action, police involvement. If the complaints procedure is not appropriate, discuss the alternatives with the complainant;

5   Consider whether the complaint could be resolved without further investigation;

6   Be aware of the timescale and the importance of speed;

7   If the complaint is about a proposed action by the department, see if the action can be deferred whilst the complaint is investigated;

8   Obtain, and if necessary secure, the relevant documents, such as files, log books and timesheets, and insist on seeing the originals, not copies, and get copies of all the documents needed;

9   Establish the relevant sequence of events from the files and also the names of the officers/Members most directly involved in the content of the complaint;

10   Analyse the complaint into its different elements for further action or decision;

11   Prepare the line of questioning for each officer;
—   use open not leading questions
—   do not express opinions in words or attitude
—   ask single not multiple questions, ie one question at a time;

12   Arrange the order of interviews so that normally followed procedures and practices are established first from more senior officers and end with those officers most directly involved in the complaint;

13   Inform all those to be interviewed that they may be accompanied by a friend or trades union representative, provided that the friend is not in a supervisory position over the interviewee. Explain the complaint clearly to them;

14   Consider whether a witness of a particularly difficult interview is needed—this is also a good way of training new investigators;

15   Interviews should be conducted in as informal and relaxed a manner as possible, but persist with questions if necessary. Do not be afraid to ask the same question twice. Make notes of each answer given;

16   Try to separate hearsay evidence from fact by asking interviewees how they know a particular fact;

17   Deal with conflicts of evidence by seeking corroborative evidence. If this is not available, consider organising a confrontation between the conflicting witnesses;

18   At the end of the interview, summarise the main points covered by the interviewee and ask if s/he has anything to add;

19   Make a formal record of the interview from the written notes as soon as possible after the interview while the memory is fresh. Never leave it longer than the next day;

20   If appropriate, visit the establishment complained about unannounced to check normal practices;

21   Draft a report setting out the evidence obtained, preferably without including opinions, and circulate this for comment to all those interviewed, including the complainant, unless there are special reasons not to do so;

22   Consider comments and amend the report as necessary, adding conclusions, and, if appropriate, a suggested remedy for the complainant;

23   Send the report with the recommendations to the DCO who will decide on further distribution as necessary.

Housing and Community Care

Introduction

1   Adequate housing has a major role to play in community care and is often the key to independent living. The Government wants housing authorities to play a full part, working together with social services departments and health authorities so that each can effectively discharge their responsibilities.

2   This circular gives guidance on the role of housing authorities in implementing the Government's community care policy following:
   (a) the White Paper 'Caring for People: Community Care in the Next Decade and Beyond' (Cm 849);
   (b) the National Health Service and Community Care Act 1990 ('the 1990 Act'); and
   (c) the Department of Health's policy guidance 'Community Care in the Next Decade and Beyond' issued in November 1990.

3   In particular housing authorities and social services authorities should be aware of:
   (a) chapter 3 section 5 in the White Paper on housing and community care;
   (b) sections 46 and 47 of the 1990 Act, which require social services authorities to consult and liaise with housing authorities over local community care plans and the assessment of individual needs;
   (c) paragraphs 1.12 and 1.13 of the Department of Health's policy guidance.

This circular expands on these and complements the Department of Health's policy guidance to social services authorities which was also sent to housing authorities. This circular is being sent to social services authorities as well as to housing authorities. The Housing Corporation will issue guidance to housing associations in due course.

Community Care

4   Community care is about providing care and support to those people who require it, for example because of the effects of ageing, physical or sensory disability, learning disability, mental illness or disorder (including dementia), alcohol or drugs misuse, or degenerative diseases such as HIV/AIDS. The aim is to support people in their own homes or in 'homely' surroundings wherever this is feasible and sensible, through the provision of the right level of intervention and support to enable them to achieve maximum independence and control over their own lives.

5   The Government's policy remains that care should be provided to people as far as possible in their existing housing where this is their preference and it is practicable and cost effective to do so. Appropriate health and social care services, where necessary in conjunction with suitably designed or adapted housing, will be key components in enabling people to live independently. For those people who cannot remain in their own homes, even with support, there will be a continuing need for other forms of housing, or residential care or nursing homes.

6   From April 1993 social services departments will assume responsibility for assessing the care and support needs of people who approach them for assistance. The planning and assessment processes which they are required to undertake, together with other agencies, should identify the full range of needs, including housing needs, of those who require care.

7   The implementation of the new community care arrangements will be accompanied by changes in the way social security benefits are paid for people in residential care and nursing homes. For those entering homes from April 1993, the Department of Social Security will no longer pay higher income support levels. Claimants will instead be eligible for normal rates of income support, as if they were living in their own homes, supplemented by a new residential allowance element. The difference between what would have been paid under the existing arrangements and the new will be transferred from the Department of Social Security's budget to local authorities. Social services authorities will therefore become responsible for meeting the costs of residential and nursing home care for people whom they assess as needing such care, whether they enter local authorities' own homes or those run by the independent sector. As now, social services departments will recover all or part of the cost by charging residents according to their means.

Community Care Planning

8   Under the 1990 Act, social services authorities have, from April 1992, had to prepare plans for the provision of community care services in their areas. Section 46 of the Act requires social services authorities to consult local housing authorities in so far as these plans affect or are affected by the availability of housing in their area.

Assessment

9   The Act also requires a more systematic assessment of the needs of those who may require care. From April 1993 social services authorities will have a statutory duty to assess individuals' need for community care services, with the aim of ensuring that all support needs are identified, not only needs for which the social services authority is responsible. Section 47 of the Act requires social services authorities to notify the local housing authority if there appears to be a housing need, and invite them to assist in the assessment. Housing needs may include adaptations, repairs or improvements to allow people to stay in their existing home. In most cases this package of services will be based on a person's existing home, but in some cases it may mean alternative accommodation.

10   Referral procedures will need to be developed and agreed locally. Both housing and social services authorities should adopt joint arrangements to deal with assessments, and should consider the need to nominate particular officers to be responsible for liaising and agreeing the possible housing options. Authorities should address the training needs of officers involved in liaison and referrals and the need for good practice guidance. Authorities should involve other agencies as appropriate.

Where adaptations or improvements are called for, referral procedures should include local Home Improvement Agencies (see Annex paragraph 10), since these agencies can play a key role in helping people have such work carried out. The process of care management and assessment is explained further in Chapter 3 of the Department of Health's policy guidance 'Community Care in the Next Decade and Beyond'.

Housing Strategies

11   Housing authorities and social services authorities are asked to co-operate fully in the planning and assessment processes, bringing in other housing providers in both the public and voluntary sectors, especially housing associations, where they may be able to help. Although for many people there will be no need for social rented housing, nor any change in their housing requirements, if additional housing needs are identified they should be taken into account in the local housing strategy.

12   As well as the generality of needs arising from the new community care arrangements to be introduced in 1993, housing strategies will need to reflect other specific needs identified in community care plans. These may include the consequences of the continuing programme of closures of long stay hospitals and the re-provision of services on a comprehensive local basis (see Annex paragraph 14). Discussions should also be held with the Housing Corporation about housing association investment in the authority's area.

13   This should all be brought together in the context of the Housing Investment Programme process, which is the subject of discussion between local housing authorities and the Department of the Environment every year. Housing authorities should draw up a picture of housing supply and need in the area and identify cost-effective and practical objectives. Consultation procedures will need to be developed and agreed locally, to ensure co-ordination.

14   It is obviously important that county social services authorities should liaise effectively with district housing authorities and, where social services and housing authorities are part of a unified authority, that discussions should take place between the respective departments. Consultation should also take place with neighbouring or regional bodies in order to establish a strategic pattern of provision wherever this makes sense. Local housing authorities should, similarly, consult social services authorities so that their area strategies can both draw from and contribute to community care planning and assessment. Housing strategies and community care plans should be consistent.

Resources

15   Both community care planning and individual assessment and care management must take account of all the costs involved, including housing and other accommodation costs, and of the resources available to the various parties, and of the other claims on such resources. In no case should the resources of any authority be committed without the agreement of that authority. The ideal solution for an

individual or group of individuals, based on a systematic assessment of needs, may not be achievable either immediately or in the near future, but it should inform the planning process. Community care in itself creates no new category of entitlement to housing, and housing needs which are identified by community care planning and individual assessments should be considered alongside existing processes and local priorities.

16   Social services authorities and housing authorities should construct an individual's care plan with the objective of preserving or restoring non-institutional living as far as possible, and of securing the most appropriate and cost-effective package of care, housing and other services that meets the person's future needs. For some people the most appropriate package of care will be in a nursing or residential home, but in many cases this will be achieved by bringing in domiciliary support and making any necessary adaptations to the individual's existing home. The balance between these should be considered carefully. For example, where expensive or disruptive adaptations or improvements are being considered it may be more cost-effective to provide domciliary care and support together with more minor works. In other cases adaptations or improvements (eg, to help people bathe or cook by themselves) may reduce or obviate the need for domiciliary support.

Review of Plans and Housing Provision

17   The impact of the new systematic assessment process will be gradual. There is no evidence to suggest that there will be immediate changes or a need for a new range of housing options. Housing authorities and social services authorities should, however, be aware of the range of new developments in housing which are becoming available, particularly in the housing association sector. In assessing the housing needs for their area in future years, housing authorities should take account of the housing needs identified in the planning process and of demographic changes in the local population, for example, the number of severely disabled people and projected increases in their population aged over 85. This should enable future planning to be based on a more comprehensive picture of an area's needs. Both local authorities and the Government will monitor developments carefully.

18   The Department of the Environment has commissioned independent research into the housing needs of elderly and disabled people, which is expected to provide guidance on key indicators for use in assessing the specialised housing needs of elderly populations. The Department expects to produce guidance to housing authorities on methods for establishing the comparative costs of different housing and care options for elderly people when the research is completed.

Working Together

19   The new proposals will require effective relationships to be established and built upon between all parties involved. The aim should be to provide a seamless service for clients, with a mutual recognition of all authorities' responsibilities. This will require all the relevant agencies, including housing, health and social services authorities, to put

an emphasis on discussion, understanding and agreement in the planning of services, rather than unilateral decision making. Joint working will be important to maximise the use of existing resources. Administrative systems will need to be developed, perhaps including existing joint planning structures, in order to monitor and plan the effective use of services. Authorities may wish to set up pilot projects. In taking forward their role in community care, housing authorities in particular should have regard to the points made in the Annex to this circular.

24 September 1992

Circular 10/92
(Department of the Environment)

LAC(92)12
(Department of Health)

Practitioner Checklist

The notes that follow are intended to provide a practical summary of some of the themes touched upon in the main text so as to guide applicant and authority lawyers if legal problems arise in respect of assessment, service provision or complaints procedures.

Stage 1   Application for Assessment

Write letter to local authority setting out prima facie need for community care services which the authority is empowered to provide/arrange for the provision of.

If the authority unlawfully refuses assessment consider:
- (a) application for leave to move for judicial review seeking mandamus (see Chapter 8); and/or
- (b) asking the Secretary of State to exercise his default powers against the authority (see Chapter 9).

Note: Option (b) will only be sensible where the authority is simply refusing to undertake assessments at all. In practice, judicial review is the means of challenge where an authority has misunderstood an applicant's eligibility criteria.

Stage 2   The Assessment

Co-operate fully in the assessment process clarifying, in writing, all contended need and the services for which need is argued.

If there are points of complaint as to how the assessment is being conducted these should be recorded in writing so as to avoid any suggestion that any breach of natural justice is being waived. If a manifestly unfair process is being operated, judicial review may be appropriate to prevent, by injunction or prohibition, the process being continued. In practice, however, the court would probably regard such application as premature.

Stage 3   The Decision

If no decision is reached within a reasonable time judicial review may be appropriate. Alternatively, and probably more appropriately in most cases, the authority's complaints procedure should be resorted to in order to resolve the matter quickly. In exceptional cases (as where the authority is simply refusing to provide a decision at all) the default powers of the Secretary of State may be sought.

If a decision is not reasoned the authority should be asked, in writing, to provide such reasons within a specified time. Judicial review should be sought if reasons are not provided.

Once a decision is made its legality or fairness may be challenged by judicial review. However, consideration should always be given to invoking the local authority's complaints procedure. If the matter is urgent, practitioners may legitimately seek judicial review because of the need for interim provision of services unless the authority agrees to provide services whilst the complaints regime is being resorted to.

If there is any uncertainty, judicial review may be sought but the application for leave may be adjourned pending the invocation of the complaints machinery. This avoids delay problems with the court and preserves an applicant's option to continue with judicial review at any time if the complaints regime is not producing results.

Stage 4   The Complaints Regime

An authority's complaints regime has three stages (see Chapter 7). The first stage is informal but, thereafter, there are strict time limits.

If the complaint is not being resolved satisfactorily, or if the time limits are breached, the applicant may seek judicial review, if the matter is urgent, without having to exhaust all the stages of the complaints procedure. If the matter is not urgent (and no interim relief is required) the court would probably expect the complaints machinery to be exhausted.

If the complaints procedure is handled unfairly or unlawfully, judicial review may be sought of the legality or fairness of that procedure. Unfairness should be protested at in writing prior to the conclusion of the procedure.

Stage 5   Tactical Considerations

At the conclusion of the process an applicant may have an action for damages at least in circumstances where an authority has made a decision in his favour but failed to provide the services in question (see Chapter 10).

The Secretary of State's default powers are exceptional and do not constitute an alternative remedy to judicial review. They should only be resorted to in an unusual case where the authority's assessment or complaints machinery has broken down.

The usual tension will be between whether to invoke an authority's complaints regime or seek judicial review. Tactically, judicial review (coupled with a claim for damages and interim relief) will often produce results. But the High Court will not lightly see the statutory complaints machinery ignored. Applicants' legal advisers should ensure that they utilise both methods unless and until it becomes apparent that one or other is likely to prove successful.

Judicial review applications must be proceeded with expeditiously. An applicant's adviser will be at risk of prejudicing the case if legal aid is not applied for quickly. However, delay in obtaining legal aid without fault on the applicant's or his advisers' part is a good reason for extending time to bring judicial review applications.

The applicant's position should at all time be recorded in writing in order to preserve maximum scope for legal argument if the matter comes before the court. Judicial review is, generally, argued solely on written evidence and letters (especially if unanswered or not answered properly) can provide valuable ammunition.

The Local Authority's Position

A local authority should ensure that its decisions are recorded in writing and that they are fully reasoned.

In community care cases maximum fairness should be shown towards an applicant to ascertain that his case is fully put.

If legal proceedings are threatened the authority should attempt to resolve the matter through its complaints procedures.

If leave to move for judicial review is sought the authority is entitled to attend court and seek to prevent: (i) leave being granted; and/or (ii) the grant of interim injunctive relief.

If leave is granted 'on the papers' without the authority's attendance it may seek to have such leave set aside if there has been material non-disclosure or if the case is otherwise unarguable. However, the setting aside procedure should be invoked sparingly.

The authority does not have to put in affidavit evidence at all. If it does so, however, it must adhere to the time limits. Failure to do so (even by one day) may result in evidence not being admitted. Any application for extension of time to adduce evidence should be made prior to the expiry of the mandatory time limit.

Discovery in judicial review is relatively rare and cross-examination almost non-existent. Applications for discovery should be carefully considered before being conceded.

If the case is compromised, reasons must be given to the Crown Office. An authority should be astute to ensure that written reasons do not create precedent for the future.

Conclusion

From the perspective of both sides judicial review is a remedy that is likely to create precedent for the future.

There is, from either side's point of view, little point in fighting a judicial review case which is likely to create such a precedent unless the merits are perceived to lie in one direction. Whilst judicial review is, undoubtedly, concerned with legality rather than merits the facts of a case not infrequently influence the court and can produce an unfortunate result.

Judicial Review Case Study

The Facts

Charles Nutfield is a patient who has been conditionally discharged from Broadmoor by the Mental Health Review Tribunal subject to a suitable residential hostel being found for him. A hostel placement has been arranged for him by his Responsible Medical Officer but the local social services authority (Sharkness) refuses to assess Mr Nutfield under the National Health Service and Community Care Act 1990, s 47, or to fund the placement by way of after care services under s 117 of the Mental Health Act 1983 because of lack of resources. It also contends that it is not responsible for him because he is not 'ordinarily resident' within the area of that authority. The authority invites Mr Nutfield to participate in its complaints procedure but he instructs solicitors to consider judicial review . . .

The Notice of Application (Form 86A) for Leave to Move

IN THE HIGH COURT OF JUSTICE   CO/

QUEEN'S BENCH DIVISION

CROWN OFFICE LIST

In the matter of an application by Charles Nutfield for leave to apply for Judicial Review (Ord 53, r 3)

And in the matter of s 117 of the Mental Health Act 1983, and s 47 of the National Health Service and Community Care Act 1990

Applicant's Ref No	Notice of Application for leave to apply for Judicial Review (Ord 53, r 3)	Crown Office Ref No

This form must be read together with Notes for Guidance obtainable from the Crown Office

To the Master of the Crown Office, Royal Courts of Justice, Strand, London WC2A 2LL

Name, address and description of applicant	Charles Nutfield Broadmoor Special Hospital Patient
Judgment, order, decision or other proceeding in respect of which relief is sought	Failure and/or refusal by the Sharkness Social Service Authority ('the authority') to (i) assess the applicant pursuant to its duties under the National Health Service and Community Care Act 1990, s 47, and/or (ii) confirm itself as having responsibility for the applicant in respect of the funding of the applicant in residential accommodation under s 117 of the Mental Health Act 1983

Relief Sought

(1) A declaration that the applicant falls within the catchment area of the authority under s 117 of the Mental Health Act 1983. Further or alternatively,

(2) A declaration that the authority is under a duty to assess the applicant pursuant to s 47(1)(a) of the National Health Service and Community Care Act 1990 and to provide after care services to the applicant, following such assessment, under s 117 of the Mental Health Act 1990. Further or alternatively,

(3) Mandamus requiring the authority to assess the applicant under s 47(1)(a) of the 1990 Act and/or to provide after care services to the applicant in the form of the funding of his placement at a suitable hostel, and/or to reach a service provision decision under s 47(1)(b) of the 1990 Act.

(4) An expedited hearing. In the event that an expedited hearing is ordered, the applicant seeks an Order abridging time for service of the authority's evidence to 14 days after service of notice of the grant of leave, or such other period as the Court thinks just.

(5) The applicant seeks an oral hearing of the application for leave.

Name and address of the applicant's solicitors or, if no solicitors acting, the address for service of the applicant	Straneway, Headless & Loveless 82 Acacia Avenue London SE15R 4AT
Signed	Dated 30 May 1993 . . . .

Grounds on Which Relief is Sought

(1)   The applicant is aged 63 and is a restricted patient detained under ss 37/41 of the Mental Health Act 1983 at Broadmoor Special Hospital.

(2)   By a decision dated 18 April 1993, the South East Thames Mental Health Review Tribunal ('the tribunal') made a decision under s 73(7) that the applicant be conditionally discharged and that such discharge be deferred pending the availability of suitable hostel accommodation subject to proper social and medical supervision as may be directed by the RMO. The tribunal considered that the applicant did not suffer from mental illness of a nature or degree that required him to be detained in hospital for treatment.

(3)   Section 73(7) of the 1983 Act provides as follows:

> A tribunal may defer a direction for the conditional discharge of a patient until such arrangements as appear to the tribunal to be necessary for that purpose have been made to their satisfaction; and where by virtue of any such deferment no direction has been given on an application or reference before the time when the patient's case comes before the tribunal on a subsequent application or reference, the previous application or reference shall be treated as one on which no direction under this section can be given.

(4)   The purpose of deferment under s 73(7) is to enable arrangements to be made to satisfy the conditions which the tribunal has attached to the patient's conditional discharge. A tribunal is not entitled to reconvene to reconsider its original decision that a patient be discharged (see *Secretary of State for the Home Department v Oxford Regional Mental Health Review Tribunal and Another* [1987] 3 All ER 8). Further, (see per Lord Bridge, p 13):

> . . . The decision should simply indicate that the direction is deferred until the necessary arrangements have been made to the satisfaction of the tribunal and specify what arrangements are required, which can normally be done, no doubt, simply by reference to the conditions to be imposed. Whoever is responsible for making the arrangements should then proceed with all reasonable expedition to do so and should bring the matter to the attention of the tribunal again as soon as practicable after it is thought that satisfactory arrangements have been made . . .

(5)   The material part of the reasoning given by the tribunal for its decision set out at paragraph (2) above reads as follows:

> It is particularly unfortunate that the RMO and the Social Worker long laboured in the belief that the relevant catchment area was Sharkness. The Tribunal is of the opinion that their belief was reasonable. Arrangements had been made, subject to the Tribunal, for a conditional discharge to the hostel in Sharkness High Street which would appear to be in every way suitable. However, it became known a few days ago that the Borough of Sharkness did not regard itself as the relevant catchment area so that the current vacancy there is to be taken up by someone else in a couple of days. Unhappily, there is no alternative hostel currently in the offing or at all known which might be suitable and

available. These circumstances are unfair to the patient and have caused the tribunal considerable dismay.

The Tribunal urges expedition in the search for a suitable hostel.

The patient made it clear, and the Tribunal accepts, that he would be willing to abide by customary conditions as may be directed by the RMO. The Social Worker . . . thought that it would not be easy to find a suitable place, but the Tribunal has no doubt that the Social Worker and the RMO will be diligent in the search. The Tribunal accepted Dr Smith's report and Dr Martin's report, which go to show the inequity on the patient of what has happened.

(6) In summary, the tribunal considered that the applicant's catchment area was Sharkness so as to entitle him to take up the offer of a place at the said hostel which was within the said catchment area. However, the authority denied and continues to deny responsibility for the applicant as falling within its catchment area. In the absence of the authority accepting such responsibility or the Court declaring that the applicant does fall within the catchment area, the applicant is prevented from taking up the offer of a place at the said hostel or any other hostel within the catchment area.

(7) The relevant catchment area is to be determined in accordance with the provisions of s 117 of the Mental Health Act 1983 which provides as follows:

(1) This section applies to persons who are detained under section 3 above, or admitted to a hospital in pursuance of a hospital order made under section 37 above, or transferred to a hospital in pursuance of a transfer direction made under section 47 or 48 above, and then cease to be detained and leave hospital.

(2) It shall be the duty of the District Health Authority and of the local social services authority to provide, in co-operation with relevant voluntary agencies, after-care services for any person to whom this section applies until such time as the District Health Authority and the local social services authority are satisfied that the person concerned is no longer in need of such services.

(3) In this section 'the District Health Authority' means the District Health Authority for the district, and 'the local social services authority' means the local social services authority for the area in which the person concerned is resident or to which he is sent on discharge by the hospital in which he was detained.

(8) The authority's understanding of its legal obligations towards the applicant is evidenced by letters from the authority as set out in the next two paragraphs.

(9) By letter dated 11 May 1993 from Miss Jane Smith, Assistant Director of the authority's social services department, to Dr Andrew Martin, the authority stated, *inter alia,* as follows:

Sharkness Social Services Department is unable to make any provision for Mr Nutfield. The London Borough of Sharkness is not allowed to expend resources on anyone other than people normally resident in the London Borough of Sharkness. Mr Nutfield is not, and never has been, normally resident in this Borough. It would, therefore, be illegal for us to support him in payment for residential care.

(10)   By further letter to Dr Martin, dated 23 May 1993 Mr MT Vessel, Assistant Director, Community Support Services, of the authority stated, *inter alia*, as follows:

> The Department is regrettably unable to offer Mr Nutfield suitable residential accommodation on the basis that he is not technically a Sharkness resident and as such does not qualify for accommodation within a special residential setting. Whilst I appreciate Mr Sharkness is occupying a hospital bed which he perhaps does not now require, I acknowledge the dilemma that you are unable to proceed until a Department of Social Services has accepted responsibility for him.

(11)   The authority has not accepted responsibility for the applicant notwithstanding the tribunal's said decision and notwithstanding continued request by the applicant's solicitors to do so.

(12)   In the applicant's submission the authority's refusal to accept responsibility for him is and was unlawful in that:

(a)   the authority is the 'local social services authority for the area to which [the applicant is being] sent on discharge by the hospital in which he was detained', (see s 117(3) of the Mental Health Act 1983, *above*) and the authority had and has a liability to maintain after care services under s 117 of the Mental Health Act 1983;

(b)   the provisions of s 117(3) aforesaid governing liability to provide after care services are disjunctive so that an applicant's lack of 'residence' in the area of a particular local social services authority cannot be decisive of the question whether an authority is required to provide such services;

(c)   accordingly, it was an error of law for the authority to confine its acceptance of legal responsibility for the applicant to the issue of 'normal residence' (though the applicant contends that, on a true construction of s 117(3), his residence in hospital qualified him as falling within the local authority's said catchment area in any event).

(13)   Further, the authority has failed and/or refused to assess the applicant pursuant to its duties so to do under s 47 of the National Health Service and Community Care Act 1990. The authority has purported to make a decision on assessment and service provision (exhibited to the affidavit sworn in support of the present application) but, in fact, the decision is one not to assess or to provide after care services because of lack of resources. No assessment has ever been undertaken and it is contended that the authority is not entitled to make a decision not to provide after care services under s 117 given that if there is a need of such services the authority is under a duty to provide them whether or not it has the resources.

Andrew Symington

Applicant's Affidavit in Support

C Nutfield:1
Applicant
Sworn: 15.3.93

IN THE HIGH COURT OF JUSTICE   CO/

QUEEN'S BENCH DIVISION

CROWN OFFICE LIST

In the matter of an application by Charles Nutfield for leave to apply for Judicial Review (Ord 53, r 3)

And in the matter of s 117 of the Mental Health Act 1983, and s 47 of the National Health Service and Community Care Act 1990

Affidavit of Charles Nutfield

I, CHARLES NUTFIELD, of Broadmoor Hospital, Crowthorne in the County of Berkshire, patient detained under the Mental Health Act 1983, MAKE OATH and say as follows:

1   I am the above-mentioned applicant. The matters deposed to herein are, unless otherwise stated, within my direct knowledge.

2   I confirm that the factual content of the notice of application (Form 86A) herein is true.

3   There is now produced and shown to me marked 'CN1' a copy of the tribunal decision referred to in paragraph (2) of Form 86A.

4   There is further produced and shown to me marked 'CN2' a copy of the documentation before the tribunal.

5   There is further produced and shown to me marked 'CN3' a copy of the correspondence passing between those persons acting on my behalf and the London Borough of Sharkness.

6   In all the circumstances I respectfully invite this Honourable Court to grant the present application. I should stress that the current hostel placement is still available for me once the local authority is prepared to undertake legal responsibility for me.

Sworn etc.

Respondent's Affidavit

J Lickspit:1
Respondent
Sworn: 1.4.93

IN THE HIGH COURT OF JUSTICE   CO/

QUEEN'S BENCH DIVISION

CROWN OFFICE LIST

In the matter of an application by Charles Nutfield for leave to apply for Judicial Review (Ord 53, r 3)

And in the matter of s 117 of the Mental Health Act 1983 and s 47 of the National Health Service and Community Care Act 1990

Affidavit of John Merrill Lickspit

I, JOHN MERRIL LICKSPIT, of Municipal Buildings, High Street, Sharkness, London SE15, Director of Social Services, MAKE OATH and say as follows:

1   I am Director of Social Services at the London Borough of Sharkness. I have read the Form 86A herein together with what purports to be a true copy of the affidavit of the applicant.

2   I make this affidavit in support of the authority's application to set aside the leave granted to the applicant by Mr Justice Blank on 5 June 1993 to apply for judicial review. The facts deposed to hereunder are true and within my direct knowledge.

3   The application for leave was granted on the basis of a purported decision of the authority which, in the applicant's contention, could not be made in law. However, the applicant has failed to exhibit the authority's subsequent decision which superseded its earlier refusal to conduct an assessment on the applicant.

4   There is now produced and shown to me marked 'JML1' a copy of the authority's said decision. I invite this Honourable Court to accept that this is a perfectly lawful decision, having assessed the applicant, not to provide funding for the applicant at the hostel given the level of the authority's resources.

5   I further invite the Court to set aside leave on the ground of material non-disclosure by the applicant as to the decision which the authority did, in fact, make.

Sworn etc.

Specimen letter seeking assessment
(exhibited to applicant's affidavit)

Straneway, Headless & Loveless
82 Acacia Avenue
London SE15R 4AT

John Lickspit
Director of Social Services
London Borough of Sharkness
Municipal Buildings
High Street
Sharkness
London SE15

26 May 1993

Dear Mr Lickspit

Re: Charles Nutfield

We are instructed on behalf of Mr Nutfield. As you will be aware we represented him at the recent Mental Health Review Tribunal hearing on 18 April 1993.

At that hearing it emerged that the London Borough of Sharkness does not consider that Mr Nutfield is the legal responsibility of your social services department. We can do no better than enclose with this letter a copy of a draft Form 86A settled by Andrew Symington of Counsel. You will see the basis of our contention that Mr Nutfield does, indeed, fall within the catchment area of your authority for the purposes of application of s 117 of the Mental Health Act 1983.

We invite you as a matter of urgency to reconsider your previous refusal to assess Mr Nutfield under the provisions of s 47 of the National Health Service and Community Care Act 1990. We are advised by Counsel that s 47 imposes a duty to assess wherever an apparent need exists in respect of community care services (of which after care services under s 117 form a part) that a local authority is empowered to provide for an applicant.

It seems clear to us that if the Mental Health Review Tribunal has ascertained a need for after care services then it would be difficult for your authority not to assess that such need exists. Further, if need does exist then it is our contention that you have a statutory duty to provide such services notwithstanding the paucity of your authority's resources.

We look forward to hearing from you as a matter of urgency, failing which judicial review proceedings will be commenced. We do not consider that your complaints machinery constitutes an adequate remedy because Mr Nutfield is already the subject of a conditional discharge from Broadmoor and arrangements should now urgently be made for a hostel placement.

Yours sincerely

Straneway, Headless & Loveless

Speciment Decision Letter
(exhibited to affidavit of Respondent)

London Borough of Sharkness
Municipal Buildings
High Street
London SE15

Adam Phipps Esq
Straneway, Headless & Loveless
82 Acacia Avenue
London SE15R 4AT

28 May 1993

Dear Mr Phipps

Re: Assessment and Service Provision Decision on Charles Nutfield

Thank you for your letter dated 26 May 1993.

As you will be aware, since receiving your letter this authority has undertaken an assessment on Mr Nutfield. I set out below the result of the assessment and decision as to service provision.

'(1)   Assessment

Sharkness Social Service Department does not consider itself the responsible authority for the purposes of application of s 117 of the Mental Health Act 1993. Nonetheless, having regard to legal argument addressed to the authority from Mr Nutfield's solicitors, the authority decided to carry out an assessment of Mr Nutfield as if it were required so to do under s 47 of the National Health Service and Community Care Act 1990.

The assessment took the form of an interview with Mr Nutfield at Broadmoor on 27 May 1993 carried out by Mr Phillip Jenkins, an administrative officer. A simple assessment of this nature was felt to be justified having regard to the fact that the Mental Health Review Tribunal had itself assessed Mr Nutfield and found need to exist for after care services. Mr Jenkins had before him all the medical reports on the applicant which were before the Mental Health Review Tribunal on 18 February 1993.

Having read the said reports and spoken to Mr Nutfield as to his wish to go to the said hostel, Mr Jenkins formed the view that the applicant was in need of after care services in the form of a hostel placement under s 117 of the Mental Health Act 1983.

(2) Service Provision Decision

The authority, notwithstanding its finding of need, did not consider that, in the light of the assessment undertaken, Mr Nutfield's needs called for the provision by the authority of community care services in the form of after care services under s 117.

This decision was reached after careful consideration of all the circumstances of the case because of the paucity of resources available to this authority and the fact that the authority has decided not to provide after care services under s 117 of the Mental Health Act 1983.'

I am sorry that I cannot give you a more favourable response. You will, of course, be aware of the existence of the authority's complaints procedures, a summary of which is enclosed.

Yours truly

Director of Social Services

Skeleton Argument for Use in Judicial Review

Chronology

Date	Event
18.4.93	Tribunal (MHRT) hearing: conditional discharge subject to hostel placement in area of Respondent, (Bundle, p 17).
26.5.93	Letter from applicant's solicitors to Respondent enclosing draft Form 86A, (Bundle, p 19).
27.5.93	Assessment conducted on applicant, (see decision letter in Bundle, p 22).
28.5.93	Assessment/Service provision decision, (ibid).

Issues

The applicant accepts that an incomplete chronology was presented in Form 86A. However, in view of the expedited hearing the respondent did not proceed with its application to set aside leave. It is the applicant's contention that the legal merits are, notwithstanding the later decision of the authority, in the applicant's favour.

The sole issue is now whether the authority is entitled to decline service provision in respect of after care services on the ground of lack of resources and/or to decline service provision because the authority has chosen not to provide such services.

Submissions of Law

Section 117 MHA 1983 imposes a clear statutory duty to provide after care services.

Having made an assessment of need the authority was, therefore, obliged to provide such services. Nothing in the assessment/service provision regime set up by the National Health Service and Community Care Act 1990 displaces that duty or converts it into a statutory discretion. Were the position otherwise the statutory duty contained in s 117 would be assimilated to a discretion (see Gordon on *Community Care Assessments: A Practical Legal Framework*, extract enclosed).

Andrew Symington

Consent to Order in Judicial Review Proceedings

IN THE HIGH COURT OF JUSTICE   CO/

QUEEN'S BENCH DIVISION

CROWN OFFICE LIST

In the matter of an application for judicial review by Charles Nutfield

And in the matter of s 117 of the Mental Health Act 1983 and s 47 of the National Health Service and Community Care Act 1990

The Applicant and the Respondent herein do hereby consent, subject to the approval of the Court, to an Order declaring that the Respondent is required to provide after care services to the applicant under s 117 of the Mental Health Act 1983, and that the Respondent do pay the costs of the applicant on a standard basis.

The reason for the making of the said Order is that s 117 of the Mental Health Act 1983 imposes a duty upon the Respondent to provide after care services and the authority has assessed the applicant as being in need of such services.

. . . .
Signed on behalf of the applicant   Signed on behalf of the respondent

Dated . . . .

INDEX